Best of Intentions

Book Four in
**The Never Miss a Sunset
Pioneer Family Series**

Jeanette Gilge

LIFEJOURNEY
BOOKS

David C. Cook Publishing Co.
Elgin, Illinois • Weston, Ontario • Torquay, England

LifeJourney Books is an imprint of David C. Cook Publishing Co.

David C. Cook Publishing Co., Elgin, Illinois 60120
David C. Cook Publishing Co., Weston, Ontario

BEST OF INTENTIONS
© 1990 by Jeanette Gilge

Edited by LoraBeth Norton
Cover illustration by Ben Wohlberg
Cover design by Dawn Lauck

First printing, 1990
Printed in the United States of America
94 93 92 91   5 4 3 2

Gilge, Jeanette.
    Best of intentions / Jeanette Gilge.
      p.   cm.
    ISBN 1-55513-611-7
    I. Title.
    PS3557.I3525B47   1990
    813´.54—dc20

                                        90-13207
                                        CIP

THE
NEVER MISS A SUNSET
PIONEER FAMILY SERIES

One

No sound from the room below. The open register in the floor beside Jeanie's bed was meant to let heat rise up to the second floor, but it carried sounds and odors as well.

Earlier Jeanie had smelled the match-sulfur when Gram lighted the fire, and a little later she smelled coffee cooking. Now there were no odors, no sounds. Gram had gone to the barn to help Uncle Roy with the milking.

Jeanie stretched her slim legs and yawned. It would be nice to stay in her cozy white bed, she thought, but even nicer to go down to the kitchen and have a few quiet moments to herself before Gram came in from the barn chattering about the weather and sharing the never-ending bits of news about her large family.

She crept downstairs and opened the door to the combination kitchen-living room that she and Gram shared. Uncle Roy, Aunt Helen, and their three children occupied the rest of the white farm house. The only sound was the soft sputter of the fire in the old black stove. No matter how hot the weather was, Gram started her day with a cup of coffee cooked in the ivory enameled pot.

Jeanie arched her back, reached as high as she could, and then touched her toes. She still couldn't put her palms flat on the floor—a goal Gram thought was silly. But then, who could imagine Gram ever being concerned about the span of her waist—at fourteen or any other age?

There was barely enough water in the water pail to splash her face, but she poured what there was into the wash basin and went to fill the pail at the pump near the back door.

Aunt Helen was busy at the far end of her own kitchen when Jeanie slipped quietly through the room. Sometimes Jeanie welcomed long talks, and even arguments, but this morning she needed a few minutes to think about the days ahead.

Squinting into the sun, she drank in the cool morning air. Two hens wandered up from the chicken coop, tut-tutting along like two amiable old ladies, until Skipper, the collie, sprang at them. They took off down the hill in a flurry of dust and a few stray feathers, cackling indignantly.

With her left arm extended to balance the weight in her right hand, she carried the water through Helen's kitchen and corner of their living room without spilling a drop—a rare accomplishment. She rewarded herself with a drink of the cold water and gazed at the big white calendar hanging on the wall beside Gram's bedroom door.

August 1, 1938! She was about to draw a line through the number one when she heard Gram coming through the house. Jeanie knew what she would say: "Such foolishness, counting days like that!" But she crossed off the day anyway, though it had hardly begun, and stared at it. She could hear Gram's heavy breathing behind her as she took off the *kopftuch* from her head and hung it up behind the stove.

Gram poured hot water from the teakettle into the wash dish, then reached for the dipper to add cold water. "Such foolishness, counting days like that. Wish you had been that anxious to go to school when you were little."

Not wanting to hear—again—the long story about how she had thrown up every morning because she was afraid to go to school when she was in first grade, Jeanie leaned toward Gram's good ear and shouted, "I'm going upstairs to get my dirty clothes."

Emma poured the dishwater into the slop pail and glanced up at the calendar. High school! The mere words set her stomach fluttering. Not one of her thirteen children had gone to high school. Of course Emmie, Jeanie's mother, had gone to what they called Normal School to learn to be a school teacher.

But the young women who went to Normal School knew what they wanted to do, Emma thought as she poured a cup of coffee and sat down at the table. These youngsters! What did they learn in high school, anyway? She buttered a piece of bread and sighed. Who knew what kind of young people Jeanie would be with?

There had been talk of Rib Lake sending out a school bus to the rural areas, but nothing was definite. If they didn't start a bus route, Jeanie's Aunt Gertie wanted her to stay with her in Ogema and go to high school with her boys. It might be good for Jeanie to be in a complete family for a while.

Emma pulled a big amber hairpin out of the pug at the back of her head and secured a stray gray lock. She hated to have Jeanie gone overnight . . . how could she stand to have her away five days out of the week? And how would she know what was happening in Jeanie's life? It was hard enough to know what Jeanie was thinking when she was home. She knew it wasn't easy for Jeanie to confide in her when she had to yell loud enough for the whole house to hear. If they were alone it might be different.

Jeanie had been three when her Uncle Roy married Helen, and Emma moved into two rooms of the farm house. Roy set up her old black Home Comfort cookstove in what had been the living room and bought a small cupboard for her dishes and groceries. She had taken the old fat-legged kitchen table and high-backed chairs, two rockers, and the corner table that stood on glass balls held by metal claws, and turned the living room into an all-purpose room.

Emma drained her cup, glanced up at the little white alarm clock that stood on top of the cupboard, and hastily cleared the table.

My goodness! What is that girl doing up there?

Emma was eager to get the washing done, as the August day promised to be another scorcher. She put more wood in the stove so the water in the reservoir would be good and hot for washing.

Lying across her bed, Jeanie turned another page in the Rib Lake high school annual she had borrowed from her cousin Myrtle. She studied the class picture of the juniors, matching each face with the name. In a school of less than two hundred, where everyone began the day at their desks in the main room, even a freshman had a good possibility of getting to know everyone else.

Gram called up through the register in the ceiling above the stove. "Jeanie! Hurry up and come down here!"

There was no use calling back, so Jeanie thumped her heel on the floor—three hard thumps which meant "I hear you!" She knew Gram could feel them more than hear them. Reluctantly, she turned the annual face down, grabbed the bushel basket that held her laundry, and ran downstairs.

"Tell you what," Gram said as she stirred boiling gloss starch with a wooden spoon. "I'll carry the hot water, and you fill the rinse tubs."

It was exactly what she always said. Jeanie rolled her eyes and headed for the pump.

Her irritation vanished as she watched the fat fluffy clouds while she pumped. It was only a dozen steps to the wash rig on the back porch. She dumped the first pailful in the galvanized tub and went back for another, unaware of Helen clearing away breakfast dishes or Marilyn and Marie, her little cousins, racing around the kitchen table.

She watched Cousin Ronnie lead Jack, the brown and white spotted Shetland pony, out of the horse barn and tie him to the garden fence. She had been five when Ronnie was born, and when they were younger they used to play together a lot. Jeanie still felt he was her ally.

Jeanie carried pail after pail after pail of water to the tub on the porch. The job could really be monotonous, but today she had plenty to think about. Just one more month and she'd actually be in high school—one place or the other! A thrill of excitement ran through her. She felt as though she already knew some of the Rib Lake teachers and kids, just from listening to Myrtle.

"Everybody likes Mr. Way. He won't put up with any goofing around, but he's a lot of fun. You'll probably have him for at least two classes. And you'll love Miss Fischer! She teaches English and Glee Club."

Jeanie had never heard of Glee Club, but she saw from the pictures in the annual that it was a singing group. She'd join that for sure—if she was good enough.

Finally the two rinse tubs were full, and Gram was already scrubbing sheets and pillowcases. Any minute now she'd say, "I'll wash the white clothes because I can stand the hot water. While I hang them, you can scrub the towels."

Gram fed a sheet through the hand wringer with her left hand and turned the crank with the right until Jeanie took over the cranking. "I'll wash the white clothes . . ." she began.

Jeanie closed her eyes and mouthed the words right with her. Did she always have to say the same thing?

For a while it was fun to scrub towels on the washboard. She scrubbed with a rhythm like Gram did—scrub . . . scrub . . . scrub . . . dunk. But when she slipped and scrubbed her knuckles—*ouch!* Too many slips and she'd have blisters.

What was really fun was washing the colored print out of flour sacks. At first the suds would be pink or blue, then they'd blend into a lovely violet. Gram had promised that she could have the next sack to make a dish towel. She would hem it on the sewing machine, stamp a pattern of a flowered cup and saucer on one corner, and embroider it. She'd give it to one of her aunts for Christmas. Or . . . maybe not! Her lips parted in a sly smile. Why not put it into the cedar chest that had belonged to her mother and start a "hope chest"? Of course, Gram would say she was too young, but she'd remind her that she was going on fifteen.

By the time Jeanie had hung the towels, Gram was done washing the aprons and dresses. She put the washboard across a tub to hold the starch pan, plunged each garment into the slimy starch, and fed them into the wringer rollers. Jeanie caught them as they came out on the other side, flat and sticky.

Gram said something about going to Aunt Ella's on Wednesday if they got the ironing done, but Jeanie barely listened. She was thinking again about what it would be like to be in school with two hundred kids instead of twenty-five.

Because there had been such little rain, Gram insisted on carrying the rinse water across the driveway and down into the garden—pail by pail.

When the next tub was nearly empty, Jeanie yelled, "We could each take a handle."

"Guess we could," Gram said and grabbed one side. Jeanie went out the door backwards, water sloshing, and together they laughed at their awkwardness.

The next morning Jeanie had the ironing board set up and irons heating on the front stove lid before Gram got in from the barn. While Gram had a cup of coffee, Jeanie ironed the pillowcases and flour sack dish towels and gave the sheets a "lick and a promise." Gram didn't see any sense in spending a lot of time ironing sheets, but she certainly was fussy when it came to dresses and blouses. Many times she insisted that Jeanie sprinkle a piece, roll it up awhile, and iron it over again if she didn't do a good enough job the first time. The ironing done to her satisfaction, Gram reminded Jeanie that they'd walk to Ella's the next day.

Ella had said she would have a lot of string beans to can, and Emma liked to help her when she could. But today she had another reason for wanting to visit her daughter: Ella knew a lot about this high school business.

Of course, Jeanie wouldn't have to board in town the way Myrtle, Ella's oldest, had done. Thank goodness for that.

Myrtle had always been sensible and seemed much older for her age. She was used to responsibility. But Jeanie? Emma shook her head. *Have to tell that child every move to make.*

After the milking was done, Emma trudged up the hill, feeling tired already. *Have to remember I'm going on seventy. Maybe I shouldn't try to walk to Ella's today. Well, I'll take it slow and stop at Al and Mamie's to rest a bit.*

Emma continued toward the house, thinking how fortunate she was to have five of her thirteen children living nearby—six if she included Roy, who was under the same roof.

Wearily Emma poured a cup of coffee and spread a slice of bread with butter and apple jelly. She was glad to see that Jeanie had already eaten breakfast.

When she finished eating, she changed her faded blue print house dress for a less faded blue dress with tiny flowers. She folded an apron and put it into her handbag. She was tying her black walking shoes when Jeanie bounced in, wearing her only pair of slacks.

Emma frowned.

"I know," Jeanie said with an impatient gesture. Then her tone changed to one of pleading. "Mama . . . all the girls wear slacks now!"

"Oh, all right! Just can't get used to girls wearing pants . . . but I guess I'll have to." She put on her shapeless old straw hat and stuck a steel knitting needle through it and her pug to keep the wind from blowing her hat away.

It was a little after nine as they walked down the first hill, the gravel scrunching beneath their feet. Jeanie ran on ahead and hung over the concrete side of the bridge until Gram caught up. All she could hear was a little trickle of water, not like in spring when the creek roared under the bridge.

At the top of the hill Gram stopped and turned around. "Always like to stop . . . and look . . . " she said breathlessly. "Barn needs painting. . . . "

Jeanie was eager to move on but occupied herself by kicking stones into the ditch.

"Stop that!" Gram scolded. "You'll wear a hole in your shoe!"

When they were down the hill and around the corner, Jeanie ran ahead to the iron bridge and hung over it, searching the depths of the copper-colored river for fish. Nothing but a few minnows.

When Emma reached the bridge, she stopped and feigned interest in the lazy stream. Her pulse throbbed in her neck, and her heart gave extra little beats as it slowed down. She should have taken Roy's offer to drive.

Emma's youngest son, Hank, lived just ahead with his wife, Beulah, and her nine-year-old daughter, Novella. Emma could see Beulah now, working in the garden. Beulah looked up and waved, and Emma slowly began to walk again.

It had taken her two years after her heart attack before she had been able to walk the two miles to Ella's. Now she wasn't about to allow her body to get weak from lack of exercise. But she hadn't thought about the heat.

Novella came running up the road to meet them, grinning broadly.

"We're on our way to Aunt Ella's," Jeanie shouted, knowing the lonely little girl would want them to stay.

But Emma gave Novella a quick hug. "Ask your mama if you can walk a ways with us."

Novella smiled up at her. "I have to get water, anyway. I'll get a pail and walk with you as far as the spring."

"Such a pretty little girl," Emma said. "A few more dimples and she'd be another Shirley Temple."

The sun beat down on her straw hat, and up ahead heat waves made the road swim. It was still a quarter-mile to the spring across from Al and Mamie's place, where Emma had promised herself a stop.

She knew Jeanie would want a little time with her cousin Ruby. "You girls run on ahead if you want to," Emma said. And as Jeanie and Novella took off, she called after, "Tell Aunt Mamie to put on the coffeepot!"

When they reached the spring, Jeanie bid Novella good-bye and headed for Al and Mamie's driveway.

Ruby saw Jeanie coming and ran to meet her, short ash-blonde hair bouncing as she ran. "We're going to Tomahawk!" she called. "You can come along!"

"No . . . Gram's behind me!" Jeanie called back. "We're on our way to Aunt Ella's."

They met, giggling as usual for no particular reason, and ran to tell Ruby's mother that Gram was coming.

Aunt Mamie was standing in her bedroom doorway fastening the belt on her navy blue going-to-town dress. She smiled fondly at Jeanie and said, with a hint of a Norwegian accent, "You're welcome to stay awhile. We're not in a hurry."

"Gram said you should put the coffeepot on!" Jeanie said with a self-conscious giggle at Gram's boldness.

Jeanie turned and saw Uncle Al sitting at the table in the dining room. He nodded and took a sip of coffee before he said, "Pretty hot for Ma to be walking today."

Jeanie shrugged. "Roy offered to take us, but she said she wanted to walk."

Uncle Al was Gram's oldest son. It wasn't as easy to talk with him as it was with the younger uncles, because he didn't laugh and tease. He usually sat in his rocker with a corncob pipe in his mouth and read or listened to the radio. But Jeanie knew he liked having her around by the way his eyes twinkled and the way he tried not to smile when he listened to their girl-talk. The way he beamed at Ruby made her wish that she had a daddy, too.

Ruby and Aunt Mamie put molasses cookies and glasses of milk on a tray. "Mama says we can take this out under the maple trees," Ruby said, leading the way outside. When they stepped out the door they saw Gram walking slowly up the driveway. Ruby handed the tray to Jeanie and ran to meet her.

With a pang of envy, Jeanie watched them walk toward the house together. Sometimes she thought if she heard, "Why can't you be like Ruby?" one more time, she'd spit! But it was true. Ruby didn't act silly. Ruby always seemed to know the right thing to do.

Jeanie settled herself in the grass to wait for her cousin. Ruby finally came and sat down beside her, smiled, and reached for a cookie.

"We're lucky Paul and Art didn't find these! Mama and I have a secret place we keep cookies in case we get company."

Jeanie finished her cookie and said, "I'm going to make the cutest dress! I saw a picture of a dress like you see Swiss or Bavarian girls wear—you know, with the lacing down the front." She made crisscrosses down her bodice with her finger. "Gram says she'll help me make one like it."

Ruby raised her eyebrows. "That'll be different."

Jeanie chattered on. "Wait till you see the material I'm going to order from Montgomery Ward! Gram said I should find something for under twenty cents a yard, but then she said I could order the lavender print for twenty-three cents. We have some white dotted Swiss for the center part."

"How are you going to lace it?

"Gram says she'll help me make thread loops, and I'll use black ribbon."

"I'll go get the catalog, and you can show me. I'm looking at some red plaid."

The two cousins had plenty to discuss.

It took a while for Emma's eyes to adjust to the light in the room when she sat down at the table with Al and Mamie. She still admired the way Al had built his "popple" house of peeled poplar logs. The logs didn't lie upon each other, but stood vertically side by side. At first the inside walls were unfinished but, little by little, he was finishing the walls with wallboard.

Emma glanced around the cozy room. Al's rocker stood beside a round table with a maroon skirt. An antique platform rocker sat next to the ornate organ.

She looked up at Mamie's smiling face as she poured coffee. "You're sure I'm not keeping you?"

They assured her they were in no hurry, and Emma relaxed and ate a cookie and sipped coffee. She was glad the girls had stayed outside. When there wasn't a lot of other talking, she could hear conversation at a table quite well.

Al brushed back his thinning iron-gray hair and wondered aloud what this Hitler fellow was going to do next. He had taken over Austria that spring.

Emma said it was all she could do to try to understand what was going on in this country without trying to understand world affairs. "I read about all these congressional acts involving millions of dollars, and I just hope that money gets where it's supposed to go."

"Oh, there's always a lot of mismanagement," Al said, "but something had to be done to help people get going again after the Depression."

"Did Roosevelt ever get that three billion for public works programs that he asked Congress for way back in April?" Mamie asked.

Al shrugged. "Come to think of it, I never did hear what happened to that. But I read awhile ago that they passed a minimum wage law for workers in interstate commerce. They're supposed to get twenty-five cents an hour minimum."

Emma shook her head. "Land's sake! A few years ago, a dollar a day was good wages."

"Yes! And that didn't mean an eight-hour day, either!" Mamie added.

Al drained his coffee cup, hooked his thumbs under his wide suspenders, and leaned back. "Don't think we've seen anything yet. Someday we'll see people earning ten dollars an hour."

"Ah . . . I can't believe that!" Emma exclaimed.

Al regarded her with a hint of a smile. "Oh, Ma! I remember when you said ordinary people would never own cars!"

Emma chuckled. "You're right! And I remember when we didn't even have a team of horses."

The sun was getting higher, and Mamie and Al wanted to go to Tomahawk. But Emma had no intention of leaving until she had talked about what was uppermost in her mind, because she respected Al's opinions. Many times she had wondered what he might have become if he had grown up in a rich city family instead of here in the north woods of Wisconsin. He could do just about anything he set his mind to—weld, build bridges, play several musical instruments—and he read continually.

Emma cleared her throat. "Are you going to let Ruby go to high school if Rib Lake sends out a bus?"

Al and Mamie looked at each other and hesitated, then Al spoke. "Well, she's almost seventeen, you know. We're afraid she might feel out of place with freshmen, but we're talking about letting her go for a year or so to take English, typing, bookkeeping—classes like that."

Emma nodded. "That sounds like a good idea." She sighed. "I know so little about high school."

Mamie laughed reassuringly. "Well, we don't know much either, but you watch! The girls will do just fine!"

Emma heaved herself to her feet. "Where are the girls? We'd better go."

Al scraped his chair away from the table. "I'm driving you. I have to take the car out, anyway." Without waiting to hear Emma's protest, he hurried outside.

"Yes, Gramma, it's too hot for you to walk," Mamie said. "I'm glad Ella's Henry always brings you home."

Emma sighed. "Have to admit I was having a little trouble today. When it's cooler, I'll walk." She shook her finger at Mamie. "I've got to keep walking, you know, or I'll get weak again."

As they chugged up the hill in Al's big old DeSoto, Emma was glad he had offered to drive.

As usual, Ella's house smelled like bread baking. "Oh, Ma!" she said, bustling across the kitchen to greet her, "I'm glad Al gave you a ride. I was wishing I had sent Henry after you."

She hurried to take a big black pan of bread out of the oven. Jeanie watched her turn three huge loaves of bread out on a dish towel and break them apart, and thought about how different Aunt Mamie and Aunt Ella looked! Aunt Mamie was all straight lines and angles; Aunt Ella all curves. She had a round body like Gram's, but her face was fuller and her smooth cheeks drew up in mounds that pushed up her glasses when she smiled. Sometimes, when she tried not to smile at the girls' silly talk, her chin got full of little dimples.

She smiled a greeting at Jeanie and told her where to find the girls, and Jeanie ran off.

Emma took off her straw hat and hung it on the deer antlers on the porch. "My land!" she exclaimed, eyeing the heaping bushel basket of beans. "I should say you do have beans!" Of course, there were plenty of people around to eat them. Ella's four big boys were home most of the time, and then there were Myrtle, Grace, and little Jim, who was almost eleven.

Emma settled herself on a low chair near the beans and took her little paring knife wrapped in newspaper out of her handbag. The knife was worn down from constant sharpening on the edge of a stone crock until it was barely two inches long. Her boys teased her that some day it would disappear right in her hand.

Ella came out on the porch wiping her hands on her apron. "Oh, Ma, come have a cup of coffee first!"

Emma shook her head. "Thanks! I just had one at Mamie's. Give me a pan so I can get started."

"There now," Ella said, after she had arranged pans and kettles for the beans. "I'll have a few minutes before I have to start dinner." She sat down wearily.

Now was the time for Emma to ask questions about high school, and she tried to think of a way to open the conversation without revealing her anxiety. But before she could say a word, Ella said, "We heard last night that the Rib Lake school board decided they can only afford one bus." She gestured with her paring knife. "And of course they have to transport the youngsters from near Rib Lake before they come way out here."

"Oh, dear." Emma rested her hands on the edge of the pan. "What will your girls do? Stay in town?"

Ella sighed. "We haven't decided. Myrtle says she can't stand to think of boarding in town one more year, and I hate to think of both of them gone all week. I just don't know."

"Gertie wants Jeanie to stay with her and go to high school with her boys."

Ella nodded. "She's talked a lot about it. You know she's always wanted a girl."

"I know, but she's such a perfectionist . . . and Jeanie's so careless."

"Ah, I wouldn't worry about that. They'll be good for each other. But what about you? Are you willing to let her go?"

Emma felt tears coming fast.

"Ma!" Myrtle called from the porch door with another load of beans. "Can you hold the door open for me?"

Emma was relieved to have a moment to compose herself before Ella sat down again.

Jeanie found Grace washing milk cans out in the pump house. She stood quietly and watched her a moment. Even in an old faded blue shirt, Grace looked pretty. Both Grace and Myrtle had dark hair, high cheek bones, and wide, friendly smiles, but there the similarity ended. Myrtle had perpetually pink cheeks and was taller and slimmer than Grace, but Grace had startling crystal-blue eyes.

Grace swished water in a milk can and poured it out. As she swung it up on the rack to drain, she saw Jeanie. "Oh, hi! Good timing!" She pushed her damp hair up off her forehead with the back of her hand. "Whew! It's getting hot. Let's go down in the woods where it's cool for a few minutes before we have to help get dinner."

Jeanie fell into step with her, and they jogged down the driveway, across the road, and into the shady woods. Jeanie found a seat on a mossy log, and Grace eased herself down so she could rest her back against a tree.

"Have you heard anything about the school bus?" Jeanie asked as soon as she could get her breath.

Grace groaned. "Yeah! They're going to buy one bus instead of two, so they can't come out this far."

"Oh, no! I was so sure. . . ."

"I s'pose you'll go and stay with Aunt Gertie."

Jeanie shrugged. "I guess so." She picked moss-covered bark off the log.

"You don't sound very excited."

"It's just that I don't know anybody there, except Clyde and Earl."

"You make friends so easily . . . that won't be a problem."

Jeanie flashed her a thank-you smile. If only she could find words to tell Grace how much it helped when she said things like that.

"What about you? Will you and Myrtle board in town?"

"I don't know. I think it would be lots of fun, but Ma doesn't like the idea of both of us being gone all week." Grace held her head up determinedly. "I know one thing! I don't want to study at home another term. I want to have some fun!"

"Me, too! I'm so bored!"

Grace snapped a twig into little pieces. "Maybe you could stay in town with us. We'd have a great time!"

Jeanie shook her head. "Gram said she'd never let me do that. She says I'm too young and giddy-headed." Jeanie sighed. "You're so lucky to be sixteen!"

Grace giggled. "And I can't wait to be eighteen like Myrtle, so I can go out without having to double-date."

The day flew by. Jeanie helped make beds, wash canning jars, set the table for dinner, wash dishes, work on the beans, peel boiled potatoes to fry for supper, set the table again, wash dishes again. . . . She didn't do that much work in a whole week at home, but she didn't mind at all, because there were other people to talk and laugh with.

That night in bed, Jeanie lay awake feeling useless and ignorant and homely. She wasn't good or pretty like Ruby. She didn't know how to run a house like Grace and Myrtle. When she was with her cousins, she felt like a little mouse—an ugly little mouse with a crooked nose.

She had been nine the winter she fell on the end of a coaster sled and hit her nose. It had been swollen and blue, but no one even thought about seeing a doctor. Later she realized that the cartilage was turned to the right and there was a bump on the bridge of it.

She didn't think a great deal about it until one day when Hank, Gram's youngest son, said, "Hey, Ma! Look at Jeanie's nose. She's getting to look just like Aunt Hulda."

Aunt Hulda! Aunt Hulda looked like a Halloween witch. Jeanie had fled up to her room and swung the hinged mirrors of her vanity dresser to an angle where she could study her profile.

Day after day she tried to force her nose straight. At night she tried to hold it that way, but she couldn't stay awake long enough to do much good.

Her only hope was that she could—what was the word Miss Hainey had used so often in eighth grade? *Compensate.* Yes, that's what she'd do. She'd exercise so she'd have the tiniest waist possible, and she'd take such good care of her skin that she'd have what Gram called a "peaches and cream complexion." And she'd keep her shoulder-length hair shiny and clean. Maybe she could make it go into a smooth, glossy pageboy like Myrtle's best friend. She could hardly wait for morning to come so she could get started. . . .

A soft evening breeze blew through the low window, and Jeanie pulled up the sheet. A car rumbled over the iron bridge, chugged up the hill by the house, and continued on up the steep grade to the west.

Jeanie sighed and whispered a prayer she had learned as a little girl. "Father, into Thy hands I commend my body and soul and all things. Let Thy holy angels be with me, that the wicked foe may have no power over me. In Jesus' name. Amen."

Emma sat on the edge of her bed and tried to settle her thoughts. She knew she should put Jeanie in God's care and not worry about where she went to school, but she couldn't bear to think of her being gone most of the week. "I'm not ready, Lord!" she whispered. "In four years I know I have to let her go, but not now! Oh, please make that Rib Lake school board do something so they can send a bus out here, so Jeanie can stay at home!"

She continued her prayers for several more minutes and then, in her silent world, she sensed God's peace.

Two

Jeanie pushed the clattery old lawn mower around the honeysuckle bush where the grass was still green, her mind swirling with questions. What would the school year hold?

As much as she wanted to go to familiar Rib Lake, staying at Aunt Gertie's would have its advantages. Aunt Gertie was full of fun; her laugh bubbled out from way down deep within. Maybe she'd teach Jeanie to cook and bake. Oh, the cakes Aunt Gertie baked!

Jeanie grimaced and yanked the mower extra hard, thinking of Gram and her "one-egg cake"—the only cake she ever baked. She dreaded the monthly ladies' church meeting because Gram would inevitably say, "Oh, I think I'll just make a one-egg cake."

"What else?" Jeanie would mumble, watching Gram stir the batter in the gray earthenware bowl. She'd pour it into a warped rectangular pan and put it in the oven, where it would run toward the front of the pan. When it was cool, she'd mix powdered sugar with cocoa and a little milk and smear it on top.

When the girls went around the heavily-laden table, filling their plates, someone would always ask which was Gram's cake . . . and Jeanie would have to point to that ugly lopsided thing, usually sitting right beside Mrs. Anderson's towering angelfood. When Jeanie grew up, she would never bake ugly, lopsided cakes!

That evening Gram came in from milking with a smile on her face. "Well," she said as she washed her hands, "it looks like you'll be going to Rib Lake after all!" She dried her hands and poured a cup of coffee.

Jeanie plopped down in the nearest chair. "What happened?" she demanded, pounding the table impatiently.

"The principal called Roy this afternoon. He said the board is asking several people to drive carloads of students to meet the bus—to save time, you know."

Gram took a sip of coffee, and Jeanie held her breath.

"Roy talked it over with Helen, and has agreed to pick up Grace, Myrtle, Ruby, Donald Johnson and Alma Zielkie. You'll meet the bus at the corner of country trunk C and highway 102."

Jeanie hopped to her feet and whirled around.

"Sit down here!" Gram said sternly. "There are a few things you have to understand! You'll be leaving early—around seven. Roy will have to have the milking done before he goes, so I'll get up and help him. That means you have to get ready while I'm in the barn. You understand?"

"Oh, yes, Mama!" Jeanie said, hugging Gram and dancing around.

She ran off to jabber with Helen, and Emma headed for the phone to call Gertie, tossing up a quick prayer on the way. "Thank You, Father! That was a fast answer!"

The wooden phone hung on the wall in Roy and Helen's living room. Emma was careful to keep the button held in while she turned the crank once to ring Central. There were thirteen other households on the party line, and most were not above listening in if they heard the slightest little "ting." A call to Central always drew an audience.

"Number, please," Central said.

"Fifty-eight," Emma answered and waited. She was glad Gertie lived in town and wasn't on a party line. One . . . two . . . three rings.

"Hello!" Gertie's voice rang loud and clear.

When Gertie had heard all the details, she said, "Well, I can't say I'm not disappointed. I thought I finally had my girl for a while . . . but I'm glad for you. I don't think you're ready to part with her right now."

The weeks before school flew by. Jeanie made a scrapbook of all the beauty articles she could find in the old copies of *Woman's Day, Ladies Home Companion, McCall's,* and *Ladies' Home Journal* that Aunt Gertie had given her. She started a new face-washing routine, and most days she brushed her hair a hundred strokes— but it still refused to go into a pageboy.

She wore her new brown oxfords around the house a little to break them in.

She could match most of the names and faces in Myrtle's annual.

After hours of ripping, re-sewing, and fussing, the lavender dress with the black ribbon lacing hung in her closet. She'd wear it the first day of school.

The morning school was to start, Emma came in from the barn and shook the rain off her sweater and *kopftuch.* Jeanie was standing by the washstand in her lavender dress and frowning at the mirror, trying to get the left side of her hair to roll under like the right side.

"Oh, Jeanie! You can't wear that dress today! It's much too summery."

Tears sprang into Jeanie's eyes. "But, Gram, I planned to wear it ever since it was finished!"

Emma gave an exasperated wave. "I know, I know! But it's just not right for such a chilly, rainy day. Go put on your brown jumper with the orange shadow-plaid blouse. That looks like fall."

Jeanie stood defiantly, fists clenched. "I want to wear this dress!"

Emma took her by the shoulders. "Look, Roy is driving out now to go get the others. You get up there this minute and change!"

Jeanie stomped upstairs and changed, muttering all the while.

She was ready and waiting, eyes on the east window, when Roy's car appeared at the hilltop. She gave Emma just the briefest peck on the cheek and ran off.

Emma sagged into her rocker, heart thumping. She had a feeling this was only the first of many, many battles of wills. "Oh, Lord, help her use her head and not do something foolish today," she whispered. Then she got up and started her day's work.

The bus was later than it was supposed to be, and Jeanie and the others had to hurry to the coat rooms and then to the main room. Mr. Ingli, the principal, was standing in front; the students were seated at their desks. When the late busload of youngsters came dashing up the stairs, he said, "Take seats as soon as possible."

Jeanie rushed into the main room. About a dozen steps from the doorway, her wet shoes slipped on the newly varnished floor, and she landed on her seat with a thump.

"Now that's what I call obedience," Mr. Ingli said with a chuckle.

Heart thumping, her cheeks burning, Jeanie scurried to a seat, trying to ignore the wave of titters that followed her.

Shakily she stowed her notebook in the desk and struggled to pay attention to what the principal was saying. Surely every eye in the room was on her!

When Jeanie came running in that evening, she knew Gram had been waiting restlessly.

"How did it go?" Gram wanted to know. She put her knitting down on her lap.

"Good, but I sure was embarrassed!" Jeanie told her about the fall, making Gram laugh. Jeanie tried to tell her a little about her teachers, but she was eager to run up to her room to play over the special scenes of her first day.

Several boys had talked to her and looked at her like she was really special, but the biggest thrill of all had been when Alan Mason, a senior with beautiful brown eyes and a slow and easy way of talking, had caught up with her in a corridor and beamed a smile down at her.

"I hear you're Myrtle's cousin," he'd said. "Good looks must run in the family!"

Jeanie didn't know what to reply.

"I'll wait for you and walk you to your first class tomorrow morning," he'd promised.

The next morning the sun was shining when Jeanie woke up. Ah! She could wear the lavender dress!

On the school bus she tried to listen to Grace, but her thoughts were on Alan. While Mr. Ingli talked in the main room, Jeanie fidgeted. She wanted to glance back and see if Alan was looking at her.

When she turned to go to class, he was still in his seat. Then he looked up and winked, and her knees went weak. Did she ever dream that a senior would flirt with her?

"Get all your homework done?" he asked in his deep velvet-toned voice.

All she could do was nod. Later she couldn't remember if she had said one sensible thing.

After supper she tried to tell Gram a few things about school while she dried dishes, but most of the things she wanted to talk about she knew Gram would call silly. She finished up quickly and got out her homework.

That night when Jeanie studied her profile in the winged mirrors, her nose didn't appear quite as crooked. Nevertheless, she would still take special care of her skin, hair . . . everything.

Then she remembered what Myrtle had said about one of the senior girls. "She certainly isn't pretty, but she's so friendly no one ever notices."

How stupid Jeanie had been to think that looks were all that mattered.

Before she crawled into bed, Jeanie knelt and prayed, "God, help me be friendly and nice and not think too much about my looks."

Jeanie woke up with a start. Saturday! She yawned and rolled over. No sense getting up right away. She wished it were a school day instead of cleaning day.

She heard Gram come in and put wood in the stove, wash her hands, and pour water into the slop pail, but still Jeanie stayed in her sleep-cocoon. Alan's brown eyes gazed deep into hers, and she heard herself asking him questions about himself with the poise of a senior. She dozed again.

"Jeanie! Get up now. It's going on ten."

Jeanie smiled at the little ivory alarm clock on her nightstand. It was exactly one minute past nine-thirty. She stretched and yawned, feeling kindly toward Gram, for whom nine-thirty was late indeed.

After breakfast she helped Gram move the rockers and corner table so they could mop the linoleum. Jeanie crawled behind the stove and washed the floor where Gram couldn't reach with the mop. She didn't mind that nearly as much as the poky job of dusting the four chairs with the little posts in the backs. She had to stick her finger, covered with a damp cloth, between each post—eight on each chair. Monotonous!

But today she had a lot to think about. She planned to rip off the white collar and cuffs from her red plaid dress, wash and iron them, baste them back on, take a walk by the river, play with little Marie, read the new *American Girl* magazine, and finish her homework.

On Sunday she sat in church on the women's side with Grace and Ruby. Gram sat behind them with Aunt Ella. Only the young wives dared to sit on the men's side with their husbands.

Try as she might, Jeanie couldn't keep her mind on the sermon. The pastor spoke so slowly that her mind went off in a dozen directions before he finished a sentence. After what seemed like an hour, he was finished.

When Jeanie saw the number of the closing hymn, she poked Grace with her elbow. They could never make it through the chorus without giggling because of Mrs. Kuhlman, who belted out every hymn and couldn't sound her "th's."

"Tousand, tousand tanks to DEEEEE. . . ." Mrs. Kuhlman would sing, and the girls would collapse.

Determined to be good, Jeanie concentrated on the words of the verse, but when the 'tousand tanks' resounded loud and clear, she felt the pew shake. By the last verse, tears were running down their faces, and even Gram's sharp tap on Jeanie's shoulder couldn't subdue her giggles. Choking, sniffing, blinking tears, the girls stood during the benediction.

Frowns awaited them.

"What on earth is the matter with you?" Gram demanded.

Aunt Ella tried to look stern, but her chin was all full of the tiny dimples that showed she was trying hard not to smile.

Aunt Mamie said, "Ruby! I will talk to you at home," but her eyes, too, danced with laughter.

That afternoon another of Gram's sons, Carl, came over for awhile with Olga and the children. Helen made coffee and put out the white luncheon cloth with the blue border and the yellow daisies embroidered on the corners. She set the table with the blue and gold china that was so thin light showed through it.

Jeanie wondered if it was Helen's way of letting Olga know that they were all still grieving over baby Rosalie's death three months before.

Jeanie sat with the grownups and had milk and cookies while the little kids ran around and yelled. After a while she went up and lay down on her bed and thought about Rosalie, born last May. The first time Jeanie saw her, she hovered over her bassinet a long while just watching her. After that she got to hold her many times. She loved to watch her pretty little face change expressions.

Rosalie was only five weeks old the day Carl stopped by to say that the baby wouldn't eat and they were taking her to Dr. McKinnon. Later that afternoon he called from the hospital and said that there was little hope that she would live.

Jeanie had been too shocked to ask what was wrong. She still didn't know. Maybe the doctors didn't either. How she had prayed and cried, but the next morning Carl had called and told them Rosalie was dead.

Lying on her bed, crying into her pillow, Jeanie recalled the funeral. At the cemetery everyone walked quietly toward the tiny open grave. The only sounds were their footsteps moving slowly across the grass and a few birds chirping. They gathered around the tiny white casket suspended over the red clay hole.

Jeanie didn't dare look at Carl and Olga. While the pastor spoke, she watched a little green worm climb over the mock orange blossoms. She choked back a sob.

Suddenly the thought struck her—*This is how Gram and the others felt when they carried my mother's casket to this spot.* For the first time she felt grief over her mother's death—the young mother she had never known. *Poor Gram! My poor dad!*

Although raising a baby alone would have been hard for him, it still must have been hard for him to give his baby to Gram to bring up. But it was what Jeanie's mom had wanted, and he honored her request.

Jeanie had never grieved for her father, either. She was ten when he died, and had only seen him four times in her life.

She placed her mock orange blossoms on the casket and stumbled blindly toward the car.

That night Gram had come upstairs and sat on the edge of Jeanie's bed. "*Liebchen*, I know how much you loved that baby—all babies." Her voice broke as she continued. "I do, too. But you know what? She won't ever have mumps or measles, or fall and skin her knees, or grieve when a loved one dies the way we're doing now! She's safe with the Lord!" Gram sighed. "But it will be a long while before we don't hurt when we think of her."

Gram had dried her eyes, blown her nose, and stood, looking around the room. "If it isn't too hot this week, we'll clean your room," she had pronounced. "Those curtains sure do need washing, and we'll take all the bedding out for a good airing!"

Staring now at those curtains waving gently in the breeze, Jeanie still wondered how Gram could turn off her emotions just like that and think of housecleaning!

She fluffed her pillow and straightened the bedspread and thought how much Olga must still miss Rosalie. She had to blow her nose, dry her eyes, and wait a few minutes before she went downstairs, where Carl and Olga were getting ready to go home. No one seemed to notice her red eyes.

Monday morning Jeanie jumped out of bed as soon as she woke up. She could see Alan's brown eyes and hear him say, "How was your weekend?" in that smooth voice that made Jeanie's heart pound. One of these days he'd ask her to go out, and she'd have to tell him she wasn't allowed to date yet. Surely he wouldn't mind waiting until spring when she'd be fifteen and could double-date.

When the first bell rang, she was so occupied checking papers in her notebook that she didn't look up until she reached Alan's desk. Every morning he had waited for her, and on Friday he had even put his arm around her as they walked to the English room.

But when she looked up this morning, his seat was empty! A pang of disappointment rushed through her.

It wasn't until after third period that she saw him walking down the corridor ahead of her with his arm around Gloria, a pretty little blonde senior. Determined not to let anyone know she was disturbed, she laughed and bantered with the other kids.

But in class she struggled to pay attention. How could Alan look at her like she was special, pay all that attention to her and then, just like that, abandon her for someone else? Her throat ached because she didn't dare cry.

While she was waiting for the school bus, Myrtle came up beside her and gave her a searching look. "Oh, Jeanie!" she said. "I'm sorry! I should have warned you. Alan and Gloria have been going steady for over a year. I suppose they had a fight, and he decided to do a little flirting."

Tears threatened to spill over. "But why?"

Myrtle shrugged, and the girls climbed onto the bus together.

"Jeanie, that's just the way things go! One day a couple is together; the next day each of them is with someone else." She smiled compassionately at Jeanie's stricken face. "You'll get used to it!"

Emma could see right away that something was wrong. The bright smile Jeanie had worn all last week had given way to a sad little frown. Emma decided to ignore it for awhile and see if Jeanie would talk, but to no avail. At supper she leaned over and tapped Jeanie's arm. "Is something wrong?"

Jeanie shook her head and tried to smile. "What makes you think something's wrong?" She hurriedly finished eating, helped with the dishes, and ran upstairs.

Emma picked up her knitting and sat down in the rocker, but she didn't knit. Instead, she rested her head against the back of the rocker and groaned. Back came that familiar thought: "You're too old for this!" A young mother would know what to do.

Tuesday morning Emma ached when she saw that the little face was still so sad. Had Jeanie done something wrong in one of her classes? Got a low grade in a test? Had someone been mean to her? If only she'd talk!

"Father," Emma whispered, "please help her with whatever it is. I don't know what to do for her."

Wednesday Jeanie tried out for Glee Club and was accepted. She smiled again. She smiled even more when she got an A on a science test.

When she got home from school, Carl was there helping Gram cut cabbage for sauerkraut. She watched Gram take off the outside leaves of a big head and cut it in half. Then Carl put the flat side down and pushed it across the wooden cutter which had a series of metal blades in the center.

Gram took the full pan of cabbage from under the cutter and substituted an empty one, then packed the cut cabbage in a stone crock and sprinkled salt on each layer. Carl carried the covered crock down to the basement while Jeanie nibbled bits of crisp cabbage and thought about how the cabbage would ferment and bubble. Just thinking of that tangy taste made her mouth water. Gram would cook pork with it, if it was available, and when it wasn't she would cook fluffy dumplings and they'd pour the juice over them and add a dab of butter. She wished it were ready right now!

The next day Mr. Ingli announced that anyone who would like to be in the band should see Mr. Speidel, the band director, after school. It would be great to wear one of those red and gray uniforms and march and play, Jeanie thought. Every Memorial Day the Rib Lake band played at school and then marched to the cemetery and played again.

Jeanie could hardly wait to ask Gram if she could get a trombone. That was what Mr. Speidel had suggested. That night when Gram came in from milking, she reported that Roy thought it would be fine for Jeanie to learn to play trombone, and she should ask Mr. Speidel to order a reconditioned instrument from the catalog. It would cost $36.00, plus a dollar for slide oil and another dollar for a lesson book, but Jeanie knew there was enough money in the bank.

When her father died, Jeanie began receiving a pension from the veterans' administration—$15.33 per month. Each month Roy wrote out a check for five dollars which Gram carefully doled out for church contributions, clothing items, gifts, and spending money. Occasionally Roy wrote a check for a mail order to Sears Roebuck or Montgomery Ward, but rarely did Gram allow the whole amount to be spent.

"Baby that slide!" Mr. Speidel instructed when it came. He showed Jeanie how to oil it and demonstrated its tone by playing a scale.

Jeanie's mouth dropped open. She never dreamed such beautiful music could come from a trombone. Nor had she realized how difficult it would be to play even one clear note! Night after night she practiced, making sure to bring her horn the day she had lessons.

Her trombone became her most prized possession, but her interest in music didn't surpass her interest in boys! A lanky boy with nice brown eyes like Alan's began saving a seat for her on the bus. For two whole weeks she was the envy of half a dozen girls—then one morning she got on and found him laughing with a blonde girl with a cute little turned-up nose.

This boy-girl business wasn't nearly as much fun as she had thought it would be. It was like playing fruit basket upset . . . only it hurt.

For Emma, autumn was a busy time. She pulled out the frozen tomato and cucumber vines and dug the carrots, then packed them in sand and put them in the cellar along with the cabbage heads that hadn't been made into sauerkraut. Garden work had grown more difficult with each season because her knees were stiff and she had to bend over from the waist. She'd have to work a little more slowly, that's all! She hadn't the slightest intention of not planting a garden next spring.

When the garden work was done, she planned to spin a skein of yarn so she could start knitting mittens for Christmas gifts.

Report card time! Jeanie slipped hers out of the envelope with trembling fingers, then let out a sigh of relief. Gram had never commented on her grade school report cards—even the fourth grade one with all A's—but, surely, her high school report card would be different. She imagined Gram nodding and smiling and saying, "I'm so pleased that you're doing so well!"

Gram was knitting, as usual, when Jeanie handed her the card. She read it carefully, nodded, and said, "Go put it on Helen and Roy's table. I don't think they're eating yet."

Was that all she was going to say? Jeanie thought of her cousin Ruby, and how Mamie and Al would beam their approval at her. She put the card on the table and came back, hoping Gram was now ready to say something.

She was. "Now, go put an apron on and get a pail of water."

Ignoring the command, Jeanie ran blindly upstairs and into her room, where she let out a sob of disappointment. *I know I'll never measure up to my mother. She must have been perfect. But I'm doing my best. I know I talk too much. I know I giggle. But can't she let me know she's glad when I get good grades?*

Emma thought Jeanie had gone to get something. She smiled as she thought, *My goodness! She really is doing well. Have to be careful not to praise her, though.*

Emma thought about the confident way Jeanie carried herself—head held high, shoulders back—much more like her dad than like sweet Emmie. That confidence could easily become arrogance.

She thought of the other homes where report cards were being read. Ella would be careful that her girls didn't get the "big head," but Mamie . . . why, she would praise Ruby right to her face! Thank goodness she was still a humble little girl. Emma sighed. She hoped Al and Mamie wouldn't spoil her.

She stirred the stew and finished setting the table. Where was that girl? "Jeanie!" she called. "What are you doing up there? Supper's almost ready."

Their days fell into a pattern, but not an entirely comfortable one. School mornings were predictably frantic.

Emma would hurry in from milking, knowing that in about twenty minutes Roy would be back from picking up the others. Jeanie would be dressed and have breakfasted, but she always had some fussing to do with her face or hair or clothes. Emma would pace around with one eye on the clock and the other on the east window where she could see the car approaching.

"Jeanie!" she'd call. "What are you doing up there? Roy will be here in five minutes!"

Then Jeanie would come down and scurry around for this or that, and the car would be coming down the hill and she'd still be hunting for something, and Emma would stand at the door with her trombone and book bag—

It made Emma tense just to think about it! "For once," she'd say, "why don't you be out there waiting, instead of making them wait for you?"

But making them wait didn't appear to bother Jeanie at all. Emma couldn't remember having trouble getting her own children out in the morning. What was wrong with the girl?

After one particularly difficult morning, Emma poured herself another cup of coffee and sat hunched over it, wondering what on earth to do.

Helen appeared and sat across from her. "Gramma!" she said without preamble. "Why don't you just let Jeanie be late tomorrow morning? Roy will get after her! She'll listen to him!"

Emma knew Helen could hear what went on every morning. "I hate to put that responsibility on Roy," she protested. "I'm so grateful that he's driving. But I do feel bad that they always have to wait for her."

Helen made a futile gesture. "Do it your way, but I think that would work." She got up and left.

Emma's thoughts turned back to Helen's suggestion many times that day. Maybe she was right. But Emma didn't want Jeanie to be scolded in front of the other girls. Maybe if she talked to Roy, told him the trouble she was having, and asked him to warn Jeanie. . . .

When Jeanie rounded the corner of the house that evening, there was the familiar overall-clad figure splitting wood.

"Hi!" she called, walking toward him.

"Ah, Jeanie! You're just the one I want to talk to," Roy said. He propped one foot up on the chopping block and leaned a blue chambray elbow on his knee. "You know, I have to really hustle to get you kids to the bus on time in the morning, and every minute counts. Suppose you could do something for me?"

Looking into his blue eyes, Jeanie nodded soberly. She adored this kindly uncle. Roy rubbed his chin, and she could hear the scratch of his whiskers. "S'pose you could talk to the other girls and tell them how much it would help if they would all be waiting for me every morning, instead of me having to wait for each of you? Donald is always there, but the girls—" He shook his head. "The bus had to wait for us three times last week."

Jeanie hung her head. "I can't very well do that until I start getting out there on time, can I?"

"Well, I guess that's so." Roy picked up another slab of wood, set it up, and deftly chopped it into sticks while Jeanie picked up an arm load of wood.

"I'll be waiting!" she called over her shoulder.

The whole bus was in an uproar when Jeanie and the rest got on the morning of October 31—they were all talking about Orson Welles' *War of the Worlds*, which had been broadcast the night before.

"My dad was even scared!" one kid said.

Another said, "Our whole family thought it was really happening, because we tuned in late."

"Yeah! They shoulda broke in a couple times and warned people," someone else said.

Jeanie felt completely left out! How she wanted a radio! Uncle Hank had had a radio when he still lived at home with Jeanie and Gram, but he took it with him when he left. Now Gram and Roy said there was no sense in getting a battery radio, because the Rural Electrification Administration would soon bring electricity to the farm homes, and then they'd get an electric one. Their electric lights were powered by a Delco generator, but that was only 32 volts and wouldn't work for a radio.

So month after month they waited for the "high line," and the world went on without their household knowing what was happening until they saw it in the paper or talked to someone else.

That night when Jeanie got out of the car, she climbed up the steep bank and ran across the lawn grumbling out loud.

"I bet I was the only kid in the whole school who didn't know what was going on," she complained to Gram.

Gram frowned. "Oh, forgoodnessakes! Such silly stuff! They'll forget all about it in two days. Now, go put an apron on!"

Three

By November, Emma could hardly remember why she had been so apprehensive about Jeanie going to high school. Though Jeanie didn't tell her many details, Emma could see she was relaxed and happy.

The object of Emma's musings burst in the door, not even bothering to take off her coat before she shouted, "Grace and Myrtle are going to the basketball game at school tonight. Can I go with them? Please?"

"How's that?" Emma said, and Jeanie repeated it even louder.

Emma looked puzzled. "Hmmm . . . how are they getting there?"

"Harvey's driving. He's going to the show. He'll drop us off at the game and pick us up after."

Harvey was one of Ella's—a good, steady boy.

Jeanie bounced on her toes, hands clasped in petition. "Oh, please, Mama! I've never seen a basketball game!"

"Well . . . I suppose. Now you dress warm—"

But Jeanie didn't stay to hear the rest. She was running to the phone to tell Grace.

The basketball game was a little bewildering. Kids yelled, the horn blared, whistles shrieked . . . but soon

Jeanie was screaming with the rest of them, cheering Rib Lake on to victory.

The gym emptied quickly once the final buzzer sounded, and the girls walked to the front door to wait for Harvey. When ten minutes had passed with no sign of him, Myrtle decided they should walk the two blocks downtown and wait at the theater.

The basketball players were coming out of the locker room, and Grace saw some boys she knew.

"Bill! Kenny! Want to walk us downtown?"

"What's the matter, scared of the bear?" asked the one called Kenny.

"Bear?" said Jeanie.

"Sure! He hangs around the field between the school and town, looking for freshmen!"

Jeanie giggled and shyly took the arm he offered her. She remembered seeing his picture in the annual, but he had looked like such a little kid she hadn't been impressed. He was still pretty short, but he didn't look like a little kid anymore—except maybe for his little pointed nose. He had a wonderful laugh that invited her to laugh with him.

The next morning Jeanie piled off the bus and almost collided with Kenny, who was standing right by the door. *My goodness, he has blue eyes!* she thought. She hadn't noticed the night before.

Smiling as if he had just heard a good joke, Kenny grabbed her trombone and said, "Need some help?"

"I have to take it over to the music room. Wait till I put my coat in the coat room." Heart thumping, she ran up the stairs. *He was waiting for me!* She couldn't get back down fast enough. When she rounded the stair landing, he turned from the window and flashed a smile that made her catch her breath.

He grabbed her hand, and they ran down the stairs and through the tunnel to the music room without talking. In quick glances Jeanie noted his wavy brown hair, heavy eyebrows, firm chin, and clear skin. He definitely was a little shorter than she . . . but he'd grow!

In the music room Kenny released her hand, set down her horn, and leaned back against the window sill. He gave her that smile again, his head cocked to the side. "How come I haven't seen you before?"

She shrugged. "Where do you sit in the main room?"

"In back."

"I'm up in front. Maybe that's why."

"You live near Grace and Myrtle?"

Jeanie nodded. "They're my cousins."

"My sister Vi and Myrtle were good friends."

"*Were* good friends?"

He laughed. "I guess they still are. Vi graduated last year. Do you know my brother, Ray?"

"I remember his picture from the annual, but I haven't talked with him." She drew circles on the wood floor with her right toe. "I remember you from the annual, too."

"Where'd you get an annual? You weren't here last year!"

She allowed herself to look up at him. "I borrowed Myrtle's."

It wasn't difficult to look him in the eye, Jeanie realized, because he didn't avoid her eyes the way some boys did. Leaning her shoulder against the window sill, she relaxed. It was like she had known him a long time.

Every morning for the next two weeks, Jeanie looked for Kenny's familiar blue and black plaid jacket as the bus pulled up to the school.

"Looks like you and little Kenny have something going," Grace observed one morning, but Jeanie shrugged.

"You know how it goes. Next week he'll probably be waiting for someone else!"

But she hoped not. She had been attracted to boys before, but Kenny was different. They never ran out of things to talk about. His dad worked in the sawmill and his mother worked at the cafe a few days a week. Vi, the sister who knew Myrtle and now worked in Chicago, was getting married soon.

Jeanie told Kenny her story, too—how her mother had died when she was only a few weeks old, and how she lived with her grandmother and had more aunts, uncles, and cousins than she could count. It was great to feel so comfortable with a boy.

At night in bed she wondered how she'd feel if Kenny abandoned her for someone else. Was it inevitable? Would he find someone more attractive, as the others had? Would she? She did wish he were taller . . . and she did go for soulful brown eyes. . . .

Emma glanced at the calendar. Less than three weeks till Christmas. Any day now the catalogue order would be here with the apron material for all the "girls." Every year she ordered several yards of percale and packages of matching bias tape. Olga and Helen wore aprons that looped over the head, but the others liked the old-fashioned kind with a back that buttoned at the waistline. It wasn't much of a gift but, Emma comforted herself, it was the thought that counted.

One gift she was sure would please—the locket Jeanie had been admiring in the Chicago Mail Order catalog. It was a little gold locket made like a photograph album and actually had pages where tiny pictures could be slipped behind little oval openings. Helen had helped her order it, and it was safely wrapped in red tissue paper and hidden in the folds of the big white tablecloth in the bottom dresser drawer.

She had knitted heavy homespun socks for her three youngest sons—Roy, Carl, and Hank. She didn't try to give gifts to all nine boys anymore. Now she still had to knit little slipper-socks for Roy and Helen's children, and she'd be ready.

At this time of the year she actually missed Hank's radio. The old thing had been crackly and squealed like a stuck pig, especially if there was a storm, but it was nice to have music at Christmas. Soon the REA would supply power to every farm home in the area, and then they could get an electric radio.

It was dark when Jeanie got home from school these December days, but there was one bright, cheery spot in the darkness—the little Christmas tree with lights out by the front porch. Roy had found twenty-four volt lights that could be used with their Delco-generated electricity. When the bus came over the hilltop, Jeanie could see the tree blazing from about a quarter of a mile away. One lonely little tree proclaiming the joy of Christmas—the only Christmas lights for miles and miles around.

On Christmas Eve day, Roy brought Gram a cedar bough and some pine branches. She put a little piece of the green cedar on the stove, and the fragrance drifted through the house while she and Jeanie stuck greens behind the pictures of Jeanie's parents that hung on either side of the north window in their oval frames.

After supper and chores, they all piled into the car and drove to the Christmas program at church. Jeanie felt odd sitting with the grownups on Christmas Eve, instead of in the front rows with the children. But it was fun to listen to the singing and recitations and not have to do anything. It was the first time, too, that she went home without a brown bag filled with nuts and candy.

As soon as the little ones were in bed, Roy brought in two Christmas trees, already in their stands—a balsam which touched the ceiling when it stood on Gram's corner table, and a larger one for his and Helen's living room.

Gram had brought the Christmas tree decorations down from the storeroom earlier in the day. Now she carried them out of her bedroom, along with a box of new candles.

Jeanie opened the box and sniffed the pleasant waxy smell.

"Be sure you put the holders on good, strong branches and see that nothing is hanging above them," Gram cautioned. She said that every year, but Jeanie didn't mind. It was the everyday repetitions that aggravated her.

"I miss Hank," she shouted in Gram's ear.

Gram nodded and smiled. "I do, too, but I'm glad he has his own home now."

On Christmas Eve Hank had never gone out with his friends. Instead he went to the church program, helped with the Christmas tree, and talked and laughed. Jeanie would sneak quick peeks at him out of the corner of her eye so he wouldn't notice, because it was so good to see him smiling and happy instead of frowning and grouchy. She thought he was the most handsome of all the uncles, with his nice straight nose and strong, dimpled chin.

But tonight it was just the two of them. Jeanie took out the pink candy beads that had been purchased by her mother and used for the school tree the last year her mother had taught.

"My goodness," Gram said when she saw them. "They're fifteen years old this Christmas."

When all the decorations were on, Jeanie said, "Can I light the candles—just for a couple minutes before we go to bed?" When Gram nodded, Jeanie lit the candles and turned off the overhead electric light. She turned the other rocker around to face the tree and gazed at the tinsel icicles twinkling in the candlelight.

"It's so beautiful!" she said, too quietly for Gram to actually hear, but Gram nodded and smiled.

Softly Jeanie sang "Silent Night." Gram watched her closely and then sang along. Tonight her hands rested in her lap instead of knitting, and she smiled a sweet, peaceful smile. The candles' glow was reflected in her glasses. Jeanie felt a rush of affection for her.

"Better blow them out now, so we have them in the morning," Gram said.

Reluctantly, Jeanie obeyed. When she leaned over to kiss Gram's cheek before going up to bed, Gram said, "Sleep good, *Liebchen*."

Tears sprang to Jeanie's eyes. She hadn't heard that for a long, long time.

Up in her room, she could still smell the fragrance of the candles. She heard Gram putting wood in the stove, Helen and Roy talking in muted tones punctuated by an occasional soft chuckle and, in the background, the hum of the telephone wires in the cold.

She should be happy. It was Christmas Eve! But there was a hollow spot inside. She was lonesome. Lonesome for Hank and lonesome, too, for that smiling boy with the laughing blue eyes—Kenny.

Teeth chattering in the cold, Jeanie pulled her old rose-colored blanket robe around her, shoved her feet into slippers, and hurried out into the dark hallway.

Helen was coming out of her bedroom, fully dressed, carrying little Marie. "Merry Christmas!" she said, and reached out to catch Marilyn before she ran downstairs. "Wait till Dad calls! He has to put wood in the stoves."

Jeanie could hear Gram putting wood in her stove, too, and suddenly the smell of wood smoke overpowered the Christmas smells of balsam and candles.

"All right . . . come on down!" Roy called, and the little feet pattered down the stairs.

Jeanie stood back with Gram and watched the little ones run for their presents from Santa. Ronnie immediately began brr-brr-ing a truck across the floor.

"Well, look at this!" Roy said, kneeling down beside him. He flipped a switch, and the little headlights went on!

"Wow! Real headlights!" Ronnie cried. He tried the switch a few times, then took off to beam the headlights into dim corners of the room.

Jeanie's eyes turned from Ronnie's delighted face to Helen and Roy, who stood with their arms linked, chuckling with delight.

Marilyn was putting a new doll into a little pink doll bed while little Marie cuddled a soft rag doll.

Jeanie almost dreaded going into their room. There wouldn't be anything from Santa for her this year—she was too old.

When the children had settled down a bit, Roy said, "Let's go watch Gram and Jeanie open their presents, then we'll open ours."

There were more presents under the tree than Jeanie had expected. When packages had come from aunts and uncles, Gram had promptly hidden them so Jeanie would be surprised on Christmas morning.

Jeanie opened a pair of pretty pink flannel pajamas from Aunt Gertie's family, and Gram opened the talcum powder Jeanie had bought for her at Zielke's store one evening after school. Talcum powder was the only cosmetic Gram ever used. She would give her nose a quick pat so it wouldn't shine and sometimes in summer, when it was hot, she'd put some on her neck.

Paper flew as Jeanie unwrapped stationery from Aunt Nora and Uncle Len. There were a nightgown and felt bedroom slippers for Gram, as well as stockings, the black tea she liked, and handkerchiefs. Then Jeanie found a tiny box from Gram. With trembling fingers she slid off the red yarn tie.

"Oh, Mama! It's just what I wanted! Thank you!" She turned the little pages of the locket. There was room for six pictures. She passed it around for everyone to see.

Then it was time to go and sit under Helen and Roy's lighted tree. Jeanie carefully blew out the candles on their tree and drew in a deep breath of the lovely fragrance. She fastened the clasp of the locket chain on her neck and ran into Roy and Helen's room.

It was good to have Roy sitting with them instead of rushing around. Jeanie loved the way Helen and Roy smiled at each other and whispered a few words now and then. Someday she'd have someone with whom to share special smiles and words that had meaning for only the two of them. Someday . . .

She wondered what Kenny was doing this morning. She could see him laughing and smiling and probably teasing his sister and brother. She wished Christmas vacation wasn't so long.

Grace and Myrtle were having an exciting holiday this year. They had a house guest, their cousin Maxine. She was in college and wanted to spend her holiday on the farm to learn how rural people kept Christmas. Jeanie was dying to meet her—she'd never seen a college girl—but Gram said she had to wait to be invited.

The day after Christmas Grace called and asked Jeanie to come and spend two nights.

"Now, you behave yourself," Gram warned. "None of that silly giggling at the table, and you be sure to help with the work. Aunt Ella will be plenty busy."

"Oh, Mama! I will," Jeanie promised. She gave Gram a quick hug and ran to pack her clothes.

Dragging her sled behind her up the last hill, Jeanie pictured Maxine wearing something bright and stylish. Her hair would be frizzy, and she'd chew gum and talk loud and tell them about lots of awful things college kids did. Jeanie planned to listen much and talk little—for a change.

Cheeks red with the cold, a bit out of breath, Jeanie opened the porch door. At the kitchen door she hesitated, took a deep breath, and knocked. Nobody knocked at Aunt Ella's. They just opened the door and called, "Anybody home?" But now she must remember to be polite.

Jeanie could hear Aunt Ella's slippers swish across the floor.

"Well, come in! You look cold! You better warm up a bit before you go upstairs and find the girls."

Jeanie had a thousand questions to ask Aunt Ella about Maxine, but before she could even get one out, she heard the girls coming down the stairs. Grace bounded into the kitchen first and gave Jeanie a quick hug. "Oh, we're going to have fun!"

Over Grace's shoulder Jeanie saw a dark-haired girl a bit shorter than Myrtle. She wore a black high-necked, long-sleeved dress. Her only jewelry was a silver pin shaped like a maple leaf. Her straight long hair was pulled back and framed her oval face in a soft, simple style.

"This is Jeanie," Myrtle said with a smile.

Maxine beamed such a warm smile at Jeanie that all her apprehension melted away. So this was a college girl!

"I've heard a lot of good things about you," Maxine said in a calm, low voice.

Jeanie sputtered, blushed, and stammered out a greeting.

"We were just going to start popping corn for popcorn balls," Myrtle said.

"We're going to have a sleigh ride tonight!" Grace added.

Jeanie groaned inwardly. What would Maxine think about smelly horses, itchy hay, cold feet—riding, riding, wondering if you were ever going to get home?

But when everyone bundled up and trooped out to the big old logging sleigh, Jeanie feigned enthusiasm. The horses plodded down the driveway, and the bells in their harnesses jingled merrily.

"Oh!" exclaimed Maxine, "I've never heard real sleigh bells! They're wonderful!"

Hmmm, Jeanie thought. *They do sound nice.*

"And the air!" Maxine continued. "It's so clear and clean, I can't get enough of it!"

Jeanie inhaled deeply. It was a good feeling.

The lights from the house became tiny dots behind them. Her cousin Harold jumped off and ran behind the sleigh to warm up. His footsteps squeaked in the cold snow, and his breath looked like a white veil flying in the wind.

They stopped to pick up Paul, Art, and Ruby, and there was much laughing and bantering. After a while everyone quieted down, and Jeanie listened to the rhythm of the horses' hooves, the bells, the quiet conversations and occasional laughter.

"I didn't know there were so many stars," she heard Maxine say to Myrtle.

Jeanie leaned her head back and gazed up at the billions of twinkling specks overhead. She hadn't paid any attention to stars for a long while.

Myrtle said, "Don't they make you feel insignificant?"

"I know," Maxine answered. "How can anyone doubt the existence of God or that He created them?"

Where Jeanie had gotten the impression that college students didn't believe in God, she wasn't sure, but it was reassuring to know this one did.

They came to a stretch in the road where snow-laden trees loomed on either side. Jeanie saw them through Maxine's eyes when the older girl said, "It's like living in a Christmas card!"

When the sleigh turned back into the driveway, she said, "Oh, this was wonderful! I didn't think I would ever actually have a sleigh ride. Thank you so much!"

Jeanie wanted to thank Harvey and Harold, too, for hitching up the horses and taking them, but no one here went around thanking people like Maxine did. Jeanie tramped into the warm kitchen without a word.

After her initial shock at discovering that Maxine was exactly the opposite of what she had expected, Jeanie felt more comfortable, but she still regarded the college girl with awe. There was something so different about her—a dignity that was reserved without being cold. *A princess among peasants*, Jeanie thought.

After the boys had gone to bed, the girls sat around the Christmas tree and talked. Maxine had some letters to write, so she went upstairs to get her things. When she came back down to the warm living room, she was wearing a teal blue velvety robe.

Jeanie watched in awe as she wrote on elegant blue note paper with white flowers down one side. Although Jeanie was not about to try to read what she wrote, she could plainly see the even rows of tiny handwriting. What a contrast from the letters Jeanie wrote to aunts and uncles with a stubby lead pencil on lined tablet paper!

Then she remembered—she had real stationery from Uncle Len and Aunt Nora! Next time she wrote a letter, she'd use a fountain pen instead of a pencil and try very hard not to make any blots.

The next day, when Maxine washed her hair, she told the girls they were welcome to use her shampoo. They watched the suds billow and sniffed the fragrance in amazement. They had never used anything but plain face soap with a bit of vinegar in the rinse water.

After they had shampooed each other's hair, Maxine brought out cotton and cold cream and asked Myrtle if she would like to have a facial.

"A facial?"

Maxine smiled. "You'll like it. You won't believe how soft and smooth your skin will be."

"Okay," Myrtle said hesitantly.

"We'll need warm water, towels, and an egg white."

"An egg white? " Myrtle and Grace said together.

Maxine nodded. "Oh, yes. It dries and tightens the skin and closes pores."

Grace and Jeanie watched as Maxine creamed Myrtle's face with her fragrant Yardley cold cream, removed the cream with wads of cotton, and spread on the slightly beaten egg white.

"Now, don't talk or laugh until it dries," she cautioned . . . which of course set Grace and Jeanie to trying to make Myrtle do just that.

When the egg white was dry, Maxine told Myrtle to splash cold water on her face to remove it.

Myrtle patted her face dry, and Maxine said, "Feel your cheek."

"Oh! It's soft as the back of a baby's hand!"

Maxine smiled. "Myrtle, why don't you give Jeanie a facial, and I'll give one to Grace?"

The cream felt lovely, but the egg white felt cold and slimy and pulled as it dried.

"You have lovely skin, Jeanie," Maxine said. "Keep on taking good care of it."

She told Grace she had wonderful bone structure—her high cheek bones would always be an asset.

They admired their glowing skin, and Jeanie asked Aunt Ella to feel how soft her face was.

"Come on, Aunt Ella! Let me give you one, too," Maxine urged, but Aunt Ella shook her head.

"Oh, not now. It's almost suppertime."

When Jeanie looked into Maxine's jar of cream, she saw that it was nearly empty.

"Your cream! We used it all up!"

Maxine smiled. "I'll get more when I go back to school."

Pulling her sled behind her on the way home, Jeanie's mind was filled with new ideas—new goals. Of course she couldn't quite imagine owning a velvet robe or Yardley cold cream. Maybe someday. But mostly what she wanted was to be as kind, generous, and quietly grateful as Maxine. Jeanie realized that if Maxine had been self-centered and stingy, all the cold cream and lovely-smelling shampoo in the world wouldn't have made them like her.

As Jeanie turned in to her driveway, another thought came: Maxine hadn't chattered nonsense. Everything she said had been worth listening to. Jeanie leaned her sled against the porch and sighed. Minding her mouth would be the most challenging goal of all.

Jeanie went back to school, and the winter stretched long before Emma. She had no trouble keeping busy, of course. It took a whole forenoon to do the washing, because she had to put on her coat and *kopftuch* every time she went to hang clothes or fetch water. Even though she used warm water for the rinse water and even warmed the clothespins in the oven, her fingers would be numb before she had hung half a dozen pieces. Later in the day, when she would take the clothes in, the seams would still be frozen stiff, but when they thawed they were nearly dry. On wash days she took an aspirin tablet for the pain in her arthritic hands.

When the ironing was done for the week, Emma was free to go to Olga's or Ella's and help them mend for a day—unless the weather was too bad for driving. She didn't attempt to walk far in winter. She didn't even go to the barn some days. In bad weather Roy would stick his head in the door and say, "Ma! You stay in today!"

"I hate not being able to help milk," she'd say, "but if I fell and broke a bone, we'd all be in trouble."

Emma hummed as she watered the geraniums, the Christmas cactus, and the red-leaf begonia on the table by the west window in her bedroom. She picked off a yellow geranium leaf and pinched back a tip on the beet-red begonia so it would sprout out on the bottom instead of getting tall and straggly. *With all the trouble in the world, should I feel so content?* she wondered.

She picked up her knitting and sat down in her rocker with a sigh. If only she could hand Jeanie a whole bundle of this contented feeling! She smiled and shook her head. *No . . . it doesn't work that way! I didn't have it handed to me, either. It came through years and years of struggles and wrong choices. She'll have to find it her own way.*

Four

The first day back to school, Jeanie jumped out of bed as soon as Gram called her. It would be fun to get back to her girlfriends and her classes—but most of all, she couldn't wait to see Kenny.

On the bus her excitement grew, and the closer they came to school the more nervous she felt. Would he be waiting? When she got off the bus, there was no blue and black jacket in sight. Her heart sank. Had he found someone else?

Jeanie walked slowly to the first floor corridor— and saw two big seniors carrying Kenny upside down by his ankles! His hair hung straight down and swayed back and forth as they strode down the hall-way. His arms were crossed over his chest—and he was laughing!

Jeanie wanted to run and make them put him down, but she stayed where she was while other kids ran after them and yelled. When they got to the end of the hall, the boys put Kenny down. He got up, brushed himself off, waved at the guys as though they had done him a favor, and ran toward Jeanie, grinning. He grabbed her trombone case with one hand and her arm with the other.

"Those guys!" Jeanie protested. "That was terrible!"

Kenny grinned and shrugged. "That's nothin' compared to what they did to me last year. One time they shoved me up the cold air vent in the main room and pushed the piano in front of it so I couldn't get out."

"What did you do?"

He chuckled. "I sat down and waited until they came back and let me out. And one time they hung me out a second floor window and told Miss Fischer if she screamed they'd drop me."

Jeanie gasped. "Weren't you terrified?"

"Naw. They're my friends. They wouldn't hurt me."

Jeanie was glad of one thing: those boys were seniors. Next year they'd be gone.

When Jeanie went for her trombone lesson the last week in January, Mr. Speidel said, "You've made real progress. Come to band practice tomorrow. Fourth period."

Gram seemed as surprised as she was—and for once she couldn't hide the fact that she was pleased. Jeanie practiced extra long that night.

A whole bunch of kids were tuning up when Jeanie got to the band room the next day. She saw a freshman girl from town with a trombone and headed toward her. Betty showed her where to sit, and Mr. Speidel gave her some music. He told them to take out "Washington Post March," tapped his baton on the music rack, gave the down-beat, and they started to play.

Jeanie barely played a note.

"Don't worry," Betty said. "You'll catch on."

That night she dreamed she was marching with the band, but she couldn't march and play at the same time.

But Betty was right . . . in a couple weeks' time, Jeanie was playing right along with the rest.

In school Jeanie had never been happier. She even forgot about her crooked nose most of the time. But at home she was miserable. It was too cold to be up in her room, so she had to read or do her homework downstairs with Gram telling her every move to make and then scolding about the way she made it.

Spring couldn't come soon enough.

Whenever Jeanie was with Grace or Myrtle that winter, their main topic of conversation was their brother Carl's upcoming wedding. They were both delighted with his wife-to-be, Elizabeth, who had an inner glow and a warmth that endeared her to the whole family.

Those weeks before the wedding were almost like looking forward to Christmas. The girls talked about the reception that would be held at Elizabeth's home and later the wedding dance at Kelly's hall in Ogema. Gram didn't like dance halls, but she had agreed that Jeanie could go with her cousins.

April fifteenth dawned clear and warm, and guests were able to spend much of the time outside. When it was chore-time, many people, including Gram, went home.

But Jeanie stayed at the reception and went to the wedding dance with her cousins Ruby, Paul, and Art. The dance was open to the public, and Jeanie hoped Kenny would be there.

There was one problem, however—Jeanie didn't know how to dance. She got flutters in her stomach every time she thought about it.

Kenny was there. Jeanie spotted his smiling face across the hall at once. He made his way toward her through the crowd.

"I was waiting for you! Wanna dance?"

Jeanie shrank back and shook her head. "I don't know how!"

Kenny's laugh rang out above the loud music. "Neither do I, but who's gonna notice? Look at this crowd. No one can move anyway!"

It was the first time Kenny had actually held her in his arms, and it was even more wonderful than she had imagined. He pressed his cheek against hers and said in a tone of voice she had never heard him use before, "You're beautiful!"

Jeanie couldn't think of a thing to say. She was used to the Kenny who dragged her down flights of stairs by one hand, who offered her a bite of his candy bar and then snatched it away, laughing at her dismay. This Kenny, breathing hard into her ear and holding her so close . . . this one made her feel like she was melting!

When Ruby said it was time to go, Kenny grabbed Jeanie's hand and they ran ahead to the car. Kenny looked like he had something special to say, but when he saw the others coming, he kissed her quickly on the cheek and ran off.

"See you Monday!" he called over his shoulder.

Trembling with excitement, Jeanie wanted to tell Ruby right away. Then she changed her mind, deciding to keep the precious moment to herself to hold close and relive over and over for days to come. Her first kiss!

In May the band practiced marching out on the streets several days a week. Jeanie felt shaky. Would she remember everything? Ray, Kenny's brother, played baritone and headed the right-hand column. Jeanie marched next to him on the left.

"Guide right!" Mr. Speidel often yelled, and Jeanie would glance to her right to see that she was even with Ray.

They were almost to the railroad tracks when Ray said, "Hey, Jeanie! You're out of step!"

She frantically tried to get back in step before Mr. Speidel saw her. How could that have happened? There now. She was in step with Ray again.

"Jeanie!" Mr. Speidel yelled. "You're out of step!"

She couldn't be! She glanced at Ray and, sure enough, she was out of step again! Near tears, she awkwardly managed to get back in. A few minutes later it happened again, and Mr. Speidel was not happy.

Knees shaking, Jeanie headed toward the band room. She dreaded hearing what he would say. Suddenly she felt an arm around her shoulders. It was Ray . . . and he was laughing! She jerked away.

"Aw, Jeanie! I was only teasing. See?" He skipped and got out of step with her, then skipped and got back in.

"Oh, you!" She tried to whack him without dropping her horn. "You tell Mr. Speidel what you did— and don't you dare do that on Memorial Day!"

One evening after school, Kenny grabbed Jeanie's hand and said, "Come on! I want you to meet my mother."

She protested, but Kenny insisted they had time before the bus came, and away they went. Kenny's house was in a row of unpainted frame houses—"company houses" that had been built by the mill. Jeanie was not impressed.

But when they walked into the gleaming red and white kitchen with the crisp white curtains, and on to the dining room, where a shining table held a crystal bowl and candlesticks, and then to the living room with more shiny tables, her attitude changed. She had never seen a house so neat and polished.

Kenny's mother greeted Jeanie warmly. She was an attractive, well-groomed lady with piercing brown eyes. She showed Jeanie Vi's wedding pictures and

they talked a few minutes, then Jeanie and Kenny
hurried back to school.

On the bus Jeanie tried to recall every detail—the
lace doilies ruffled like a clown's collar on several
tables, the spotless white cupboards in the kitchen, the
wicker "fernery" filled with graceful Boston ferns.
Those sharp brown eyes bothered her a bit—she had a
feeling they could blaze with anger—but she concentrated on the friendly smile. *I think she liked me*, Jeanie
told herself.

On Memorial Day morning, Emma and Jeanie got
ready to go to the ceremony. Jeanie polished her black
shoes and put on the new black socks Mr. Speidel had
instructed them to wear. Emma had to help her tie her
black necktie.

Watching her march in the red and gray uniform,
looking so grown up, Emma's eyes filled. *I wish Emmie
could see her*, she thought, as she always did when
something special happened in Jeanie's life.

"Why, that's your little girl, isn't it?" a neighbor
said in Emma's ear as the trombone section led the
way into the cemetery. Emma nodded and beamed.

"You must be so proud of her!" the lady shouted.

Again Emma nodded and smiled. "Oh, yes, but I
certainly don't let her know. Don't want her to get the
big head."

The neighbor nodded in agreement.

After Memorial Day, summer stretched ahead like a
desert. There was gardening to do and berry picking
and sometimes the girls would stay overnight with
each other . . . otherwise it looked dismal.

About a week after school was out, Jeanie went to
the mailbox and found a letter from Kenny! She tore it
open and struggled to read the penciled writing on
glossy white paper.

Dear Jeanie,

*I hope you are having a good vacation. I
went fishing a couple times. Didn't catch
much. I'm bat boy for the baseball team, so I
get to go all over to the games.*

*Would it be all right if I rode my bike
out some day? My Mother says it's fine
with her. Ask your Gramma.*

Jeanie flew into the house, thankful that she had
often talked to Gram about Kenny. Waving the letter,
she shouted, "Kenny wants to ride out here on his bike
someday. He wants to know if it's all right with you."

Gram put down her knitting. "He wants to ride a
bike out here? Fourteen miles on these bumpy old
gravel roads, up those big hills?"

Jeanie nodded vigorously.

Gram sighed, shook her head, and resumed knitting.
"These kids! Well . . . you'll have to help me plan what
to feed the boy."

Jeanie gave her a quick hug, let out a whoop, and
ran upstairs to write to Kenny and say he was welcome
to come the following Wednesday. Back came a letter
saying he'd be there in the forenoon.

That week it didn't bother Jeanie a bit to dust between all those little posts on the chairs and help with
the other cleaning. She helped Gram make a macaroni
and cheese casserole, and Gram let her bake a chocolate cake.

Jeanie was glad girls could wear slacks now. She'd
feel more comfortable showing Kenny around the farm
in slacks than in a skirt. Her only pair was navy blue,
and she decided to wear a red and white checked
blouse with them.

On Wednesday she looked out of the west window
a thousand times and made three trips down the hill to

the outhouse, while the clock hands seemed to stand still.

Finally, there he was! He rode straight back to the tool shed where Roy was working, hopped off his bike, and extended his hand to Roy. Jeanie watched a minute from Helen's kitchen window before she went out.

She felt self-conscious now, out of the school atmosphere, and Kenny wasn't quite as exuberant either.

"Come meet Gram," she said, leading the way around the house rather than going through Helen and Roy's kitchen. Gram was coming in from the garden with a handful of radishes. She didn't offer to shake hands, but motioned for Kenny to go ahead of her into the house. "How did you make those hills?" she asked, talking loudly as usual.

Kenny appeared a bit startled.

Oh, dear, thought Jeanie. *I forgot to warn him.*

He hesitated a moment, then took a step closer to her and shouted, "I didn't have any trouble. I'm used to riding up hills."

Jeanie brought him a glass of water. She certainly didn't expect him to drink out of the dipper the way farm people did. He drank it without stopping, grinned, and handed her the glass.

After the first few awkward minutes, they talked freely, just as they did at school. Hand in hand they ran all over the farm. After dinner Gram said she'd do the dishes, and they walked down to the river.

Jeanie showed him the spot she called "the park," where the cows kept the grass so short it looked like a lawn and elderberry bushes provided natural landscaping under the towering elm trees.

Kenny leaped from one big boulder to the other across the river. "Come on!"

Jeanie shook her head. "Oh, no! I'm not part monkey like you are!"

Feigning anger, he sprang to the bank, as agile as a squirrel on a limb, and pretended to choke her. Laughing gaily, hands clasped, they strolled to the footbridge—two railroad tracks suspended across the river. The rails were stable at the end, but by the time the two of them got to the middle, their footsteps had set the rails bouncing. Jeanie squealed and Kenny grasped her arm as they made their way to the other side.

She showed him a good fishing hole and told him how they used to net suckers in the spring. Then they went back over the footbridge and up the gentle slope to the pile of rocks that marked the spot where the old log house, where Gram and her husband had started their married life, had once stood. She thought of showing him where Gram's little stillborn baby was buried, but decided not to go into that long story today. They cut across the field through the stony area, and she showed him a boulder that sparkled with mica and told him how she used to pretend it was diamonds.

When they got back, Helen was on the porch swing. She was pleasant enough, but Jeanie couldn't help feeling that Helen didn't approve of Kenny coming to spend the day or of the way they ran all over the place.

They played tag with the little kids awhile, then went into the house and had chocolate cake and milk. Kenny glanced up at the clock that stood on top of the cupboard. "Gee! I gotta go."

He shouted "thank you" and "goodbye" in Gram's ear.

Jeanie walked with him to his bike, wishing he'd kiss her again, but he must have been as aware as she was of all the eyes on them.

"Maybe I'll ride out again sometime," he said. "Okay?"

Jeanie nodded and smiled, then walked around to the west end of the house so she could watch him pedal up the long hill till he was out of sight.

When Jeanie walked into the kitchen and slammed the door behind her, Gram looked up from peeling potatoes and flashed a bright smile. "Did you have a good time?"

Jeanie smiled and nodded.

"Nice boy," Gram said. "He looks a person right in the eye. Now, run down in the cellar and get a jar of green beans."

Jeanie knew the conversation was ended. Gram wouldn't be interested in a detailed account of their time together. Sighing, she went to get the beans. It would have been fun to tell her where they had gone and what they had talked about.

Emma finished the potatoes and glanced at the clock. Too early to start boiling them. She hadn't been sure if Kenny was staying for supper or not.

She sat down and picked up her knitting. Had she done the right thing in allowing him to come? They were so young. Helen disapproved, she knew. Maybe she should have asked Ella's opinion. But Jeanie was fifteen now—old enough to have boyfriends. Of course, she wouldn't let her run off with a boy in a car—at least until next year.

There was so much she should tell the child, but how to start? It seemed like her own girls had learned what they needed to know—somehow. After all, talking too much about these things only made young people more curious.

She chuckled to herself. What was she worrying about? This little Kenny . . . he was certainly harmless! She had been glad when Jeanie told her he was German. They were probably good, hard-working people.

Oh, forgoodnessakes! she chided herself. *Next week there will probably be a different boy in Jeanie's life. It's not like she's going to marry him.*

Now it was haying season. Jeanie wished she could be out on the hay load like Ronnie, but Gram didn't want her to milk cows or do other farm work. She never wanted it said that they had made a farmhand out of Jeanie. Jeanie herself never could understand Gram's fear—after all, her father's relatives never came near. But at haying time, there was something Jeanie was allowed to do.

A load of hay was coming. Jeanie could hear the horses plodding up the hill behind the barn and hear the wagon creaking under its load.

Helen stopped sweeping the kitchen and went to the cellar for cool homemade root beer for Roy to drink. Jeanie ran to the barn as Roy drove the horses and loaded wagon into the "thresh" floor. He unhitched the horses and took them around to the rear of the wagon.

After a quick drink of root beer, he climbed up on the load, grabbed a rope, and pulled the big hay fork along the track suspended from the barn roof until the latch clicked. With an overhand motion he pulled the rope down, down until the hay fork was suspended over the load. He plunged it deep into the hay, then jumped on it to drive it deeper. Then he pulled up the levers which opened blades deep in the hay to secure the load and stepped aside.

Helen drove the horses up the hill a bit, attached a heavy hemp rope with a hook on the end to the single-tree and, with a snap of the reins, drove the horses up the slope.

The big rope grew taut and, as the horses pulled, the hayfork and its load lifted up, up to the roof of the barn, as pulleys creaked and the old barn groaned.

Jeanie held her breath as it climbed. It struck the latch with a clang, and the load sailed down the track with a sound like distant thunder. When it reached the spot where Roy wanted it to fall, he gave the rope a smart yank, pulling in the blades. The hay fell off the fork with a heavy thud.

Now it was Jeanie's turn. Helen had unhooked the big rope that had pulled up the load, and it had to be pulled back to the thresh floor so it could be rehooked for the next load. Jeanie pulled and pulled, hearing the rope thud on the thresh floor with each pull, until it was all back and ready to use again.

It felt good to be able to do something. The days went faster when she had one ear tuned to an approaching hay load.

In the middle of August, Kenny rode out on his bike again. She knew he was coming and was thinking of little else, but Gram had forgotten. That morning when Jeanie mentioned it, Gram said, "Oh, forgoodnessakes! Ella called yesterday and asked if I'd come and help her can pickles. Henry's going to come and get me. I thought you'd come along."

"But, Ma! I can't!"

"Well . . . you behave yourself. There are frankfurters in the cellar, and there should be a ripe tomato or two, and there's plenty of sweet corn. Now, have the water boiling before you even go and pick the corn. Sweet corn has to be fresh to be good."

Kenny came before Gram left, but it didn't seem to bother her to leave them. Jeanie knew Helen didn't approve.

Time went fast until after dinner. Kenny had been all around the farm, so there wasn't much left to see . . . and he said that he didn't have to leave until seven. Oh, dear! What would she cook for supper? Well . . . they could always go to Aunt Ella's.

Out in the back yard Jeanie said, "We used to climb that big spruce tree by the driveway, and we could see Uncle Henry and Aunt Ella's barn from up there. They're a mile away—straight through the woods."

"Do you ever walk over there through the woods?"

Jeanie shook her head. "I haven't, but Gram says there used to be a path through there years ago."

Kenny's eyes twinkled. "Want to try it?"

Jeanie giggled. "Why not?"

She called to Helen and told her where they were going, but didn't wait to hear her reply.

After dinner Ella insisted that Emma take her half-hour nap, just as she did at home. It felt good to stretch out after sitting all forenoon. It was almost four years since she had lain in this bed after her heart attack, Emma realized. It had been a slow climb back to health, but she had recovered.

After her nap, Emma sliced cucumbers for bread and butter pickles and Ella worked at the stove.

Grace came in from the garden with another bucket heaping with cucumbers. "I think that's all," she said, wiping her forehead on the roller towel by the wash stand.

She took a deep breath. "Ahh . . . if this is what a pickle factory smells like," she shouted in Emma's ear, "I wouldn't mind living next to one."

Emma smiled and nodded. The freshly sliced cucumbers, mingling with vinegar and spices simmering on the stove, certainly did smell good.

Grace bent down to shout in her grandmother's ear again. "So Jeanie's boyfriend rode out on his bike again today!"

Emma chuckled. "Well, it's kinda hard for me to think of little Kenny as a boyfriend. It's more like she's running around with one of the cousins."

Grace laughed. "Gram, I don't think any of her cousins would ride fourteen miles on gravel roads up all those hills to come and see her!"

Emma's smile vanished. "I suppose not."

Grace went to the cellar to get more canning jars, leaving Emma to her worries. She rested her arms on the edge of the pan and looked thoughtfully at Ella. "I'm wondering if I did the right thing leaving Jeanie and Kenny on their own. They seem like such little kids. . . ."

Ella smiled. "Tell you what. Why don't I call and invite them over for supper?"

"That would be fine, but last time he left in the afternoon."

"I'll call and see," Ella said and cranked out two long rings and two short ones.

"Hello, Helen. Is Jeanie there? . . . Oh. I see. . . . What time did they leave?"

She sat down, leaned toward Emma, and shouted, "Helen says they're on their way over here—through the woods."

"Oh, forgoodnessakes! Through the woods! There's no trail there anymore. Those crazy kids!"

"Oh, Ma, they'll be all right. They can't go far without coming out at a road."

Ella chattered while they worked—about Helen's and Beulah's new babies, both due in the fall, about the school bus that would be coming all the way to their homes this year, about Carl's plans to build a new house—but Emma barely replied. Her thoughts were on those two in the woods.

The first quarter of the way through the woods was no problem. Jeanie had been back in the woods berry picking and knew where an old logging road was, but suddenly they were facing nothing but solid woods.

When they came to a fence, Kenny stepped on the lowest strand of barbed wire and lifted the top two. Jeanie slipped through and then held them for him.

"This must be the end of our farm. That means we're halfway there."

"What's to the south?"

"Woods, at least for half a mile, but we'd run into Rocky Creek if we went south."

"What's north?"

Jeanie laughed. "Woods! What else? At least a quarter of a mile. There's one farm on that corner of the section."

They tried to walk straight, but they came to a swampy section and had to go around. They came to another fence and, eventually, to one more. It didn't seem like they would ever come out at the road.

Most of the time Kenny went ahead and made a way through brushy spots, but now and then, when it was clear enough, they walked side by side. Jeanie loved the sense of adventure.

"Look!" Jeanie said. "Doesn't it look lighter over there? Maybe that's the road."

They came out a bit west of Aunt Ella's house. When they arrived panting on the back porch, full of stickers, flushed and sweaty, Aunt Ella beamed a smile at them. "Well, come on in. Looks like you could use a drink."

Emma heaved a sigh of relief. "It took you long enough. Did you get lost?"

"Not really," Jeanie shouted. "I think we went in circles a little when we tried to get around the swamp. But it was fun!"

Ella beckoned to Jeanie. "Would you like to stay for supper?" she whispered.

Jeanie giggled and nodded vigorously. "Kenny doesn't have to leave until seven. I didn't know what to fix for supper!"

At the table Kenny mentioned that they went through three fences, and Cousin Harvey laughed. "You kids sure must have been going in circles. There's only one fence between here and Roy's!"

After a good chicken supper, Uncle Henry drove them home.

When Kenny was ready to leave he said, "Hop up on the handlebars, and I'll give you a ride up to the fence line."

Jeanie got on the handlebars, and they rode out of the driveway. "I can hardly even make this grade by myself! How do you do it?"

"I didn't get off the bike once riding out here," he said.

When she got off the bike, she wanted to tell him she was glad he came, but she couldn't get a word out and couldn't tear her eyes away from his. He leaned closer and closer and kissed her—and not on the cheek, either!

Jeanie watched him until he got to the top of the hill. Then she strolled home.

Oh, how she wished school were starting tomorrow!

Five

One evening, a few days before school started, Gram sat in her rocker knitting while Jeanie trotted back and forth between the wash stand and the bench that held the water pail. First she held a hot wash cloth over her face to open pores, then she lathered her face with suds like a man about to shave and made tiny circles with her fingertips. Next she used warm water to rinse her face and, finally, a cold water rinse.

"Forgoodnessakes!" Emma scolded. "You scrub your face like it was a dirty old boot!"

Jeanie dried her face and stomped upstairs. If it wasn't Gram crabbing at her, it was Helen. Just the other day Helen had accused her of being vain because she was always looking in the mirror.

"I am not vain!" she had shouted back at Helen. If Helen only knew what Jeanie thought when she looked in the mirror!

Mouse! she spat at the face looking back at her now in the hinged mirrors in her bedroom. *You have a face like a little mouse! No one would take a second look at you!*

She didn't have vivid blue eyes like Grace, or striking black hair and rosy cheeks like Myrtle, or a lovely smile like Ruby. And all three of them had straight noses!

The closer it came to the first day of school, the more nervous she grew. Maybe this year she'd be able to make friends with some town kids besides Kenny. Not that she wanted another boyfriend . . . but it would be nice to know what other kids were talking about in their little circles.

The morning of the first day, Gram came in from the barn and said, "Jeanie, you run around like a chicken with its head cut off! Settle down!"

Jeanie was all too familiar with that awful sight—the chopping block, the fluttering, squawking chicken held firmly in Roy's hand. One deft blow of the axe, and the headless chicken would flop and roll with blood spurting from the neck. Ugh! She shook her head and tried to blot out the awful image.

She combed her hair for the third time, lined up her book bag, lunch, and trombone case, and walked out to the east end of the porch to watch for the bus. This year the route had been extended to their neighborhood.

What would it be like to be a sophomore? Who would she turn to with her questions, now that Myrtle had graduated? Would she like typing class? Would Kenny be waiting for her?

The bus finally came into view. Heart pounding, Jeanie grabbed her things and gave Gram a peck on the cheek.

Kenny was nowhere around when Jeanie got off the bus. She stopped and talked to Pearl, who was also a sophomore. Jeanie liked Pearl, who was as careful as Jeanie was careless. Her dark brown pageboy never separated. Her notebooks never had loose pages sticking out of them. Her desk was always neat.

"Did you see Kenny during the summer?" Pearl asked.

Jeanie told her how he had ridden his bike out to see her twice.

"You two are such a special couple. I hope you never break up, " Pearl replied.

Just then Jeanie saw Kenny walking toward the door between two tall classmates. He'd be sixteen in a few weeks. Surely he'd start growing pretty soon.

Laughing as always, he threatened to mess up Pearl's hair, then grabbed Jeanie's trombone case and headed toward the music room.

Jeanie felt as though a huge spring had suddenly been released inside her. She skipped along beside him.

"Hey! I'm an uncle!" he announced. "My sister had a baby girl the day I was out to see you—August 18."

"You're an uncle!" The contrast with her six-foot uncles made her giggle. "What did they name her?"

"Merle Ann!"

"Hmmm . . . that's different. I like it."

Kenny leaned back, his elbows on the window sill. "She'll probably be half grown up before I see her. I wish they didn't live in Chicago."

On September 15, Hank came in grinning from ear to ear. "It's a girl!" he announced. "Beulah had a pretty rough time. Doc McKinnon had to use instruments. But everybody's okay."

"Have you named her?" Emma asked.

"Greta," Hank replied, and was gone.

Emma smiled to herself all day. Imagine Hank with a child of his own!

The fall work was more difficult than ever, but Emma was determined not to ask for help. Helen had all she could take care of herself, with a baby due in a few weeks.

Emma wondered how things were going between Jeanie and Kenny, but Jeanie never confided in her. Her one-word responses to Emma's questions brought conversation to a quick halt.

As Emma picked the last ripe tomatoes and the largest green ones, she thought how glad she was that Kenny wasn't driving yet. How she dreaded that time when Jeanie would go off with some boy in a car. Accidents could happen so quickly with these young, inexperienced drivers. She prayed a quick prayer in advance. *Father, protect Jeanie. Keep her from ever being injured in a car accident.*

Typing class was the worst part of Jeanie's day. At first it had been fun, but as the weeks went by, she struggled more and more. No matter how hard she tried, she did horribly on the accuracy tests. And it didn't help a bit to hear Mary, the girl behind her, clicking smoothly along as though she'd been born typing.

Her other classes made up for it, though. On the school bus each evening, Jeanie's mind whirled with new thoughts accumulated throughout the day. She was glad she had Mr. Way for biology. Sometimes he'd talk about the future—about inventions Jeanie could hardly imagine. He told them that at the New York World's Fair, which had been in progress since the end of April, there was a display that showed how pictures could be picked up and shown on a screen right in your own home! He said it would probably be a few years before it could be manufactured cheaply enough for most people to own one, but he was sure that the day would come. Jeanie thought about that a lot. It would be like having a movie theater in your own living room.

Though the school district now owned two buses, Jeanie's bus still made a short local route before her route, so she had time after school to run around. She wished Kenny weren't so sports-minded. Their after-school time together would end when basketball season started. About once a week they'd walk down to Schultz's on Main Street, and Kenny would buy her an ice cream cone or she'd treat him.

The evening of October fourth, Roy poked his head in the doorway to say that the baby was coming. Dr. McKinnon was on his way, and Roy was going to fetch Aunt Clara, who would help Helen out for a couple weeks. Clara had been Gram's friend for years, even before she married Gram's brother Walter.

At bedtime Jeanie tiptoed past Helen's closed bedroom into her own room and shut her door. She wasn't sure she wanted to hear anything that went on. Hours went by. She could hear Dr. McKinnon's voice and, now and then, sounds like Helen was lifting something or doing hard work. Then a baby's cry! What a beautiful sound! She heard someone say, "It's a boy!" and she went to sleep.

The next morning she was able to take a peek at baby Arne. He had dark hair and fat cheeks and was kind of red.

Because the door between the rooms was rarely closed, Ronnie, Marilyn, and Marie ran in and out at will. During the day, when the older two were in school, Gram spent quite a bit of time amusing little Marie.

Jeanie helped carry food trays to Helen. It was odd to see active Helen in bed, but even with dark circles under her eyes, she was pretty. On the eighth day Aunt Clara said Helen could sit up and dangle her feet over the edge of the bed, and on the tenth day she could stand.

Jeanie remembered when Helen's other babies had been born, but she hadn't been aware of the whole process or really thought about what it would be like. Now she realized there was a great deal she didn't know about having babies. In spite of growing up on a farm, she'd never even seen a calf born—Gram had made sure of that.

Jeanie asked Aunt Clara a few questions, but her curt answers discouraged further questioning. And there no point in asking Helen—Jeanie knew she didn't even talk to Gram about such things. She even tried to find something in the school library, but without success.

About a week after Arne was born, Jeanie closed the door between the rooms and pulled her rocker next to Gram's. Close to Gram's ear she said, "What's it like to have a baby?"

Gram drew back, as shocked as if Jeanie had announced that she were going to have one! She coughed, brushed some lint off her navy blue dress, and scowled. "Land's sake, you don't have to know about things like that at your age! You'll know soon enough."

In bed that night, Jeanie wondered why she felt so guilty for wondering. What was wrong with having a baby? Wasn't it a natural thing? You'd think after giving birth fourteen times, Gram wouldn't be so uncomfortable talking about it.

But having a baby remained a mysterious, scary business. How would she ever have the courage to have one herself?

One afternoon, while Helen was still upstairs and the baby and little Marie were asleep, Emma invited Clara to come and have a cup of tea. She closed the door so their talking wouldn't disturb the others.

"Ahh! Good!" Clara said, as she sipped the hot drink. "I admit I'm a bit tired. Two weeks is long enough. I'll be glad to get back home."

"I don't know how I could have run up and down stairs all the time the way you have," Emma said, grateful for Clara's help. She was tempted to tell Clara how much she resembled Eleanor Roosevelt, but she wasn't sure Clara would be flattered.

"You know, Emma, you've come a long way these last four years. My goodness! We thought you were going to die that day at Henry and Ella's anniversary celebration!"

Emma nodded. "I did, too." She took a sip of tea. "But something happened to me through that experience. I was always so worried that I might not live until Jeanie was through school. But after that close call, I just knew that the Lord would keep me going until Jeanie doesn't need me anymore."

Clara smiled. "Jeanie is getting to be a lovely young lady."

"Yes, she's growing up. But I wish she weren't so giddy-headed! She'd forget her head if it weren't on tight!" She pointed to a pile of underwear on the table. "I bet I've told her five times to take those things upstairs!"

Clara chuckled. "I know you have! You don't realize how loud you talk, Emma."

Emma's face flushed. "Oh, my! I didn't realize you could hear me way in there."

"You know," Clara said seriously, "Jeanie's no different from any other teenager. When your children were growing up, you had too many people around to notice what each one of them did or didn't do. But with only Jeanie to look after, you watch her like a hawk!"

Emma thought about what Clara had said. Maybe Jeanie wasn't any worse than most teenagers, but Emma felt a weight of responsibility she had never felt with her own children. She meant to work hard to see that this little girl grew up to be a good woman—a humble woman. Emmie had never been so talkative or so concerned about her appearance.

Jeanie and her cousins Grace and Ruby loved to talk about how it would be when they were grown up. They discussed who they would marry, how many children they would have, and where they would live (close enough to visit each other regularly, of course).

Now Jeanie wondered if they actually would live near each other. She had never thought there would be a time she wouldn't see Myrtle frequently, but now her older cousin was working in Lake Geneva and only came home a few times a year. Jeanie looked forward to Christmas, when Myrtle would be home. Jeanie had dozens of questions to ask her, and she knew Myrtle wouldn't be embarrassed. She wouldn't laugh, either, no matter how stupid those questions were.

Sometimes Myrtle would tell her what she remembered about her mother. Myrtle had been four and a half when Emmie died, but she remembered how beautiful she had looked laid out in the pink georgette dress with rose buds pinned between the tufts of the casket lining.

"You look a lot like her," Myrtle had said once.

Jeanie sighed. "Gram says I certainly don't act like her! I talk too much."

Myrtle smiled. "I remember Emmie giggling and chattering, just like us!"

"Do you really?"

Myrtle nodded.

"I want so much to be like her! She was kind and loving and thoughtful and—"

Impulsively, Myrtle hugged her cousin. "I think you'll be a lot like her. I know you will be!"

Jeanie relived that conversation often. She would think about what Myrtle said, not what Gram said.

For Jeanie, the winter months of 1940 were as exciting as cold dishwater. "It's the same old thing day after day," she grumbled to herself. "Get up in the dark, run downstairs and dress by the stove, try to find something different to wear, ride the bus over the same old roads, look at the same dirty old snowbanks and the same pimply-faced boys. If only I were old enough to date."

Kenny, Pearl, Grace, and a few others were the only bright spots in her life, although Pearl and Grace were always talking about their problems with boyfriends. At least she didn't have fights with Kenny. She never felt depressed when she was with him—how could anyone not feel good around those laughing blue eyes?

But back home, as soon as Jeanie stuck her head in the door, Gram would say, "Now, go and put an apron on!" and Jeanie would feel like running back outside. In a way she was glad Gram's hearing wasn't good—it meant Jeanie could mutter a lot of things that Gram couldn't hear!

Although Gram's every-day-the-same remarks got on her nerves at night, it was the morning weather report and steady stream of talk about family members that really got to Jeanie. It drove her to do quickly whatever she had to do downstairs and flee back to her room. But it was cold up there—so cold that the water she took upstairs for setting her hair at night was often frozen by morning. She couldn't stay there long.

For Emma, on the other hand, the winter months were a haze of comfortable days. Once Jeanie was out of the house, she spent a few minutes in prayer and then got to work. When she had finished sweeping and setting her rooms to order, she'd work on a patch-work quilt or a rag rug or her ever present knitting. "Can't sit idle," she'd often say. She couldn't actually hear the teakettle sing or the fire snap anymore, but in her memory she still relished those peaceful sounds.

She could have been unhappy, alone in her quiet world, if she allowed her mind to dwell on Jeanie's shortcomings. Had her other children really been as forgetful, self-centered, and careless? But in those quiet times, Emma sang hymns and let the precious words lift her spirit. How long would it be, she wondered, until Jeanie, too, would know this peace?

Actually she felt a bit sorry for Jeanie this winter. Grace and Ruby, who were two years older, were already going out on dates, while Jeanie sat home weekend after weekend. Emma knew she longed to be with other young people. At times Emma longed to put her arms around the child and comfort her, but fear of losing control over Jeanie held her back. Rearing a teenager was like driving a high-spirited team of horses—one had to keep a firm grip on the reins.

Saturday morning Jeanie stood by the north window, cleaning rag in hand. She stared at the worn-out snow that had repeatedly melted a bit and frozen again until it was almost as gray as the sky and the bare box elders. There wasn't a thing to look forward to this weekend. She pictured Grace, Ruby, Pearl— every girl she knew—getting dressed for a date or maybe a party. Even playing Monopoly at someone's home would be fun.

She felt Gram's hand on her shoulder and started.

"Ah, *Liebchen,*" Gram said sympathetically, "spring will come. Then you'll have many things to be excited about."

Liebchen! Jeanie caught her breath. Gram did care! It was like sunshine bursting through the clouds. She wanted to pull the rockers close together and pour her heart out . . . but when she turned, Gram was wringing the mop, pointing to where she wanted a chair moved. There wasn't a hint of softness in her face.

Anger welled up in her throat, and Jeanie slammed the chairs into place. "All she ever cares about is cleaning, not how a person feels!"

The third week in February, Jeanie flew into the house, cheeks flushed with excitement. Carefully she closed the door between their room and Helen's living room and urged Gram to sit down in her rocker. She pulled the other rocker close and grabbed a pencil and paper.

Kenny asked me to go to the PROM! she scribbled.

"Prom?" Gram said as loud as usual.

Jeanie put her finger to her lips. Helen disapproved of dancing.

"What's a prom?" Gram whispered almost loud enough to be heard through the closed door.

Jeanie wrote frantically. *It's like a party—a dance at school. The girls wear long dresses and the boys wear suits. They elect a king and queen.*

Gram's lips moved as she read it. "Hmmm . . ." She frowned. "This is at school?" she whispered.

Jeanie nodded.

"How would you get there?"

Jeanie wrote, *Grace is going with Spike—Kenny's friend. He drives. We'd go together.*

Gram was still frowning. "When is this?"

April 26.

Gram waved her hand. "Lots of time yet. We'll see."

But I have to get a dress—buy one or make one.

"There's plenty of time. Now, go put an apron on. . . . "

Gram got up and put wood in the stove, and Jeanie dropped the scribbled notes into the fire. Gram would go to Aunt Ella's this week, for sure. She always did when she had something to talk over. Jeanie smiled to herself. Aunt Ella would tell her it was all right.

The following Wednesday, when Jeanie came home from school, Gram whispered, "I talked to Ella today.

She says Myrtle went to the prom twice and it was real nice. Of course, some kids went out drinking afterwards." She shook her finger at Jeanie. "You find out what those boys plan to do. If they're going out to a tavern afterward, you're not going!"

"Oh, they wouldn't do that!" Jeanie said, right in Gram's ear.

"Well, then, we better think about your dress."

On Sunday Carl and Olga invited Gram and Jeanie for dinner. Jeanie helped Olga set the big dining room table. Potatoes bubbled merrily on the stove, and the venison roast smelled wonderful. Gram sang little German songs to five-year-old Gladys and four-year-old Marvin. Albert, who considered himself a big boy at seven, looked on.

Jeanie loved this little log house—and the people in it! It was so good to be able to talk to Olga without shouting. She babbled on about the prom.

"Gram says we better make my dress, but she's never sewn a prom dress before. What color do you think it should be?"

After the dinner dishes were washed, Olga pulled out the mail order catalogs, and they pored over pages of fabric and ready-made dresses.

"Looks like net is the most popular material," Olga said. "How about pink net over pink taffeta?"

Gram sat near them looking lost.

Olga leaned toward her. "Would you like me to help her sew it?" she shouted.

"Oh, my goodness, I sure would!" Gram said with a sigh of relief.

Three weeks later Jeanie hiked over to Olga's with the bag of material and a pattern. Together they cleared the big table and laid out the beautiful soft pink taffeta. All the while they worked, they talked about all the things Jeanie would have liked to talk about with Gram, if she'd been able to hear . . . and if she'd have been interested.

Without lecturing, Olga let Jeanie know how she felt about drinking and about how to act with a boyfriend. "What is a big thrill one time will be old stuff the next, "she said. She laughed and shook her finger at Jeanie. "Ration those kisses!" By the time Jeanie had to go home, the dress had taken shape. Lace with black velvet ribbon drawn through it would accent the neckline. That would come last.

Walking home, Jeanie thought about their conversation. She was sure Olga was right about rationing kisses. One thing she knew—she would never "have to get married." Now and then there were whispers about some girl, and it made Jeanie feel ill. Olga said that a bride's white gown stood for purity. Jeanie knew that someday she'd wear a white gown and walk down that aisle knowing she had a right to wear it.

Weeks before the prom, Jeanie's dress hung finished in her wardrobe. Several times she had gone with Kenny to visit his mother, who seemed almost as excited as the kids about the prom.

But they hadn't counted on one thing—sinkholes! When the frost came out of the ground, the dirt roads broke up. When that happened, sinkholes of soft mud had to be skirted. In some places, planks had to be laid over them. People drove their cars as little as possible. Sometimes they met at a bad hole and transferred milk, mail, and groceries by foot around the bad spots.

It looked like prom week would find the roads at their worst. With just two days to go, the bus driver announced that he would not be driving down county trunk YY. If anyone wanted to go to school, they would have to meet the bus at the intersection of YY and 102. There was no way the boys would be able to drive out to pick up the girls for the prom on Friday.

"It's not the end of the world, "Gram said. "You can always wear your dress next year."

Next year! Jeanie glared at Gram's back.

On Thursday Roy drove Jeanie to meet the bus. That morning Kenny was all smiles.

"My mother says you and Grace should bring your dresses to school tomorrow and get dressed at our house. You can stay overnight, and we'll take you home Saturday after I'm done with my paper route. All you gotta do is get someone to take you to the bus, like you did this morning."

When Jeanie told Gram, she shook her head. "But I don't even know Kenny's mother!"

"What difference does that make?" Jeanie asked.

Gram studied Jeanie's eager face a moment. "Oh, all right. Call Grace and see if one of the boys will drive tomorrow morning."

The gym didn't even look like the gym with all the Hawaiian decorations and soft lights. Jeanie still didn't know how to dance, but she wasn't as nervous as she had been at Carl's wedding. It was fun just to see all the pretty dresses and be so close to Kenny and smell the pink and white carnations in the corsage he had bought her.

When the music ended, he still held her close. "You're beautiful!" he whispered, just the way he had at the wedding. A thrill of excitement swept through Jeanie. Surely tonight he'd kiss her again.

When the dance ended, Kenny and Jeanie joined Grace and Spike. "I told my mother we wouldn't be home till daylight," Kenny said.

Jeanie's eyes grew round. "Daylight!"

"Sure," Grace said. "It's prom night. We have to do something special."

Kenny's eyes twinkled. "How about driving down to Rib Mountain and watching the sun come up?"

Jeanie gasped. "But that's sixty miles away!"

"Aw, what the heck!" Spike said. "Let's do it."

Jeanie dozed a bit on Kenny's shoulder on the way to Wausau. They had bacon and eggs at an all-night cafe and then drove up to the state park. Another carload of kids from the prom were already there. They had found a wheelbarrow and were giving each other rides—even the girls!

"I'm not getting in that thing!" Jeanie told Kenny.

"You don't have to," he assured her.

Suddenly a spotlight was on them. Cops! They stood squinting into the light while an officer strode toward them.

A boy from the other carload explained that it was prom night, and they were going to watch the sun come up.

"All right," the cop said with a smile. "But no drinking! And whoever is driving better have a cup of coffee before you head back. Can't sleep and drive, you know."

"I didn't know policemen could be so nice," Jeanie whispered to Kenny.

Drifting in a blissful haze as they rode home, Jeanie looked up into Kenny's eyes. Those eyes, usually full of laughter and mischief, were serious now—tender—adoring.

He drew in a quick breath. "I love you!" he whispered.

Her heart all but spilled out of her as she whispered back, "I love you!"

At the end of an embrace that left them breathless, she remembered Olga's warning about rationing kisses. Deep within herself, Jeanie chuckled. Olga had to be kidding!

When they drove into town, men were going to work in the mill and Kenny's mother was sitting at the kitchen table reading the paper. She offered to make breakfast, but Jeanie and Grace said all they wanted to do was sleep. She showed them upstairs to a bed with a fluffy down comforter. Poor Kenny had to change clothes and go do his paper route.

Snuggled deep in the soft bed, Jeanie was still in an ecstatic world she hadn't know existed until tonight. Kenny loved her! It was fun to flirt and see other boys' admiring eyes, but that was nothing compared to the thrill she felt now.

Home again, Jeanie told Gram and Helen about their all-night escapade—how much fun it had been and how kind the police officer was. She wasn't prepared for their shocked response—especially Helen's. She thought staying out all night was terrible!

Jeanie crept off to bed feeling like a punctured balloon.

"But we didn't do anything wrong!" Jeanie insisted, when she and Gram were alone the next day. She didn't feel a bit guilty about the tender kisses. "I just don't understand. . . ." She started to cry.

Gram patted her hand. "There, now, *Liebchen*. Don't feel bad. Just remember—sometimes people will try to make you feel guilty about something because it *looks* like it could have been bad. But if you know you didn't do anything wrong"—she gave a little wave—"just forget about it!" She smiled roguishly. "I'm glad I didn't know what you kids were going to do. I would have had to forbid it."

Emma toured the front yard, searching for signs of new life and gathering twigs until her apron could hardly hold them. Back in the house, she fed the twigs into the fire. Northern Wisconsin springs had a way of playing peek-a-boo. One day the early April sun warmed the moist earth until it steamed; the next day a sharp wind blew and icy rain pelted until one could almost see the new sprouts shrinking back into the ground.

She went back outside and smiled up at the warming rays of the sun. Then her eyes searched the south side of the woodshed for dandelions. Yes . . . there were several. In the shed she found cardboard boxes and set them over the dandelions, as she had for more years than she wanted to count. In a few days they'd make a tangy salad.

Her eyes wandered down to the umbrella-shaped elms along the river. They were showing a hint of green, and the willow brush down in the swamp was yellow. The violets wouldn't be blooming yet, but she'd take a little walk across the west field to the stone piles. Surely there would be mayflowers.

It seemed like such a little while ago that Jeanie was with her on these walks, tugging at her skirt or running ahead to find "fowers." When she was a child, she had delighted in every little thing. Now it seemed she sought only what was new and different. Emma sighed. *She misses so much by not enjoying the little things right in front of her.*

Most of the time Jeanie hated that long bus ride. But now it was spring, and on a day like this, her eyes drank in the shimmering green of new tree leaves and searched for tiny spring flowers.

The sun was actually shining by the time she got on the bus these days. This May morning she took mental photographs of the light rays probing deep between the trees—right to the very floor of the forest. When the leaves grew dense, only spots of sun could get through, but now, as though to make the most of that precious sun, plants grew so fast that each day new colors appeared. Just the other day she had seen the first trilliums, just a sprinkling of white here and there, and now they virtually carpeted the woods.

She pretended she was taking pictures for post cards and aimed her imaginary camera at a lovely curve of white birch lining the road, the sparkling water of Spirit Lake in the background. When she filled her eyes with such beautiful scenes in the morning, they would flash back in her mind's eye throughout the entire day, restoring each time a little of the original pleasure and peace she felt at seeing them.

Yes, she was really fortunate, she decided, in spite of the tiresome bus ride. Town kids didn't get to see the blazing autumn colors, or the white-frosting mornings when every twig wore white fluff, or the flower-carpeted woods in spring.

Emma picked clusters of pale mauve and pink mayflowers to put in the toothpick holder on the center of the table. As she strolled back toward the house, her thoughts, as usual, were on Jeanie. *Two more years and she'll be out of school. Where have those years gone?*

Tears blurred her vision. Jeanie didn't know what she would do after graduation, but she would certainly not be content to stay home. And why should she? What was there for her here?

Emma tried to imagine life without her. Oh, yes, these were trying years, no doubt about it. But it was tremendously rewarding, too, to watch this young life unfold.

Father, I can't bear to think of her leaving. Help me get used to the idea of letting her go. Help me to turn my attention to others—to something to fill the empty space when she goes.

Six

When school let out the first week of June, Jeanie felt like she could sleep twenty-four hours a day. She had been the household grass-cutter for quite a few years, but this summer she had to rest and rest before she could finish the lawn.

"What's the matter with you, girl?" Gram asked one day when Jeanie carried in a pail of water.

Out of breath, Jeanie plopped into the rocker. "I'm so tired! I just don't feel well."

Gram felt her forehead. "You don't have a fever."

"I'm not sick," Jeanie said impatiently. "I'm just so tired!"

A few days later Jeanie found herself in Dr. McKinnon's cluttered office. He thumped her back and peered into her eyes, ears, nose, and throat. "Oh, yes! My, my!" He turned to Emma and shouted. "Bad tonsils! Like poison to her. She'll have to have them out."

He suggested they stay at Uncle John's in Park Falls and have the operation at the hospital there. Then he handed Jeanie a bottle of tonic and said, "When you get those tonsils out, you'll feel like a new person!"

She certainly hoped so. Now, lying in a cold hospital bed, staring out the window at nothing, she wished it were all over. The strong antiseptic smell made Jeanie's stomach feel sick. The nurses and doctor were all pleasant, but they did little to allay her nervousness. When they came to put Jeanie on a cart and roll her into the operating room, she felt a rush of real fear. Then the mush of ether gauze covered her face, and the next thing she knew she was back in her room crying—not for Gram, but for Kenny!

She stayed in the hospital that pain-filled night and tottered to the car the next morning when Aunt Esther and Gram came to get her. Cousin Jean brought her magazines to read and went to the store for ice cream, but Jeanie could hardly talk. Aunt Esther's chicken noodle soup burned so badly it brought tears to Jeanie's eyes. Uncle John's cheerful jokes didn't help, either.

It was good to get home to her own bed that night, but she was so miserable she didn't want to do anything. The only bright spot on her horizon was Kenny's promised visit on Sunday—though she hated for him to see her like this.

He drove out alone, proud to have his license. He didn't stay long, but his short visit was better than medicine. When he was leaving he leaned over the lawn lounge, kissed Jeanie gently, and whispered, "I love you."

Long after he was gone she heard those precious words and whispered, "Oh, Kenny. I love you, too!"

Jeanie thought she must have just a little idea of how Myrtle must be feeling. She had met a young man named Harry in Lake Geneva, and Grace had hinted that Myrtle was really serious about him.

Lying on the lawn lounge, looking up at the glossy leaves and patches of blue sky, Jeanie dreamed of Myrtle's wedding—and of her own! Two more years of high school, and then—there was nothing she wanted to do except get married and have her own house and babies!

As soon as Myrtle's wedding was announced, Jeanie began work on an aqua dress with a full skirt and a sweetheart neckline to wear to the wedding. It was exciting to think of Myrtle getting married, but it was also a little sad. The overnights of storytelling and giggling were gone for good.

By the time school started, Jeanie had recovered from her operation, but she still felt weak in the knees after climbing a flight of stairs. For the most part she ignored the weakness and tried to keep up with Kenny.

On September fifteenth, Jeanie held her breath as Myrtle came down the aisle, radiant in her white satin gown and carrying white gladioluses. What was she thinking? Jeanie wondered. What would it be like to walk down the aisle to be joined to a man for the rest of your life?

After the ceremony in the little white church, the guests drove to Uncle Henry and Aunt Ella's place. But instead of feeling excited and happy, Jeanie had a sense of apprehension. It was like living the day of Gram's heart attack all over again—the same yard, the same time of year—many of the same people—the first colored leaves. It was foolish to think it could happen again, she told herself, but she kept an eye on Gram nonetheless.

Jeanie joined Grace and several other girls upstairs. They sewed Myrtle's nightgown shut, so that her head would only go as far as the waistline, and tied some of her clothes in tight knots and giggled at the thought of her trying to open them.

It seemed to Jeanie that the whole countryside turned out to the wedding dance at Kelly's hall that evening—including Kenny, of course. It was wonderful to dance with her cheek close to his and to watch the colorful wedding party.

Afterward he talked his brother, Ray, and Ray's girlfriend into driving Jeanie home. Jeanie and Kenny found themselves in the back seat, as they had been after the prom night. There was no counting the kisses this time.

As usual, Jeanie gently bumped Gram's bed when she got home. They both knew she couldn't shout in the middle of the night, so Gram would ask questions and Jeanie would nod or shake her head and say a word or two right in her ear.

"Did you have a good time?"

Vigorous nod.

"Did Ella's boys bring you home?"

Vigorous shake.

"Who brought you home?"

"Kenny and his brother and girlfriend."

"Oh . . . that was nice."

Emma stayed awake a long while after Jeanie went upstairs. Soon Kenny would be coming for her, and they would go off alone. She trusted their intentions . . . it was human nature she didn't trust.

It was quite a while before she could pray, *Father, I put her into Your care. I can't be with her wherever she goes, but You can.*

Jeanie was awake a long time, too. She could see Myrtle, her hair darker than ever against the white veil and her always-rosy cheeks almost the color as the bridesmaids' gladioluses. The girls had looked lovely in deep fall colors of wine and rust.

A fall wedding was pretty, but Jeanie decided she'd like a spring wedding with delicate colors. She could see herself carrying a bouquet of lily-of-the-valley that would tremble with each step she took. How she loved their fragrance.

Back in school Monday, she told Pearl all about the wedding and the dreams of her own.

"Think you'll marry Kenny?" Pearl asked.

Jeanie felt her face flush. "Who knows? I might!"

In November Kenny announced that he was an uncle again. Vi had had a little boy, Arthur Jr. Lots of people had babies a year apart, so Jeanie wasn't really surprised.

Hank and his wife, Buelah, had moved to town so Hank wouldn't have to drive so far to work. Now when there were band concerts or basketball games, Jeanie stayed overnight in Rib Lake with them.

One night, when Kenny walked Jeanie home to Hank's house on Main Street, they stopped on the sidewalk to kiss goodnight. Jeanie looked up, and there was Charlie Dodge, the village cop, right behind Kenny! He just chuckled and told Kenny not to be late with his newspaper the next morning.

The first week of Christmas vacation, Grace phoned to invite Jeanie to a tobogganing party at Stone Lake. The big boys had made a packed-snow slide down the hillside by the lake.

When Jeanie told Gram, she frowned and said, "In this weather? It's below zero!"

"But, Ma . . . Grace is going!"

"Well, you're not! Go and call Grace and tell her that!"

Jeanie did as she was told. "Grace? Ma says I can't go—but you know how she always gives in. I'll call you back."

Jeanie didn't beg, just went about her work . . . stopping now and then to wipe her eyes or sniff.

"Those kids are crazy to go out on a night like this!" Gram muttered.

"There's no wind!" Jeanie stated matter-of-factly.

"But it's still cold! You'd freeze your feet. You don't have snow boots—just those rubber overshoes."

"I could wear lots of socks!"

Emma chewed her bottom lip. If only it weren't so cold!

"There's a cottage right there on the lake where we have chili and popcorn and stuff. If I get cold, I can always go in and warm up!' Jeanie yelled in Gram's ear.

Gram sighed and rolled her eyes. "It's against my better judgment, but if you dress warm and—"

Jeanie didn't hear any more. She was on her way to the phone.

"Grace? I told you she'd give in!"

It was cold! In spite of her three pair of socks, Jeanie's feet were numb before they even got to the lake. The socks made her shoes feel awfully tight.

Elaine Blomberg, a classmate from school, was already there, and she and Jeanie started out across the lake toward the lanterns the boys had set up.

"I thought it wasn't windy," Jeanie gasped through the wool scarf across her face.

It was a long climb up the hill, and then they had to wait a while for their turn. They stomped their feet and swung their arms trying to keep warm.

When they were loaded on the toboggan, arms around each other's knees, someone yelled, "Let 'er go!" Away they went, down, down the slide so fast Jeanie couldn't get her breath, and ended up out on the lake.

"Man! That was great!" someone yelled, and someone else said, "We set a record! Look how far we went!"

But Jeanie grabbed Elaine's arm. "Are you going back up again? I can't feel my feet."

"Me, either! Let's go to the cottage and warm up."

They headed toward the faint light across the lake on feet that felt like stumps.

In the cottage they fell into chairs, pulled off their overshoes and shoes, and stuck their numb feet up against the jacket of the stove.

"Oh, my feet!" Elaine pulled them back from the stove and rubbed them frantically.

"Ow!" Jeanie yowled. "Oh, they hurt! I've had cold feet before, but never like this!"

Elaine tried walking to see if that would help, and Jeanie limped after her. They cried, then laughed at how silly they looked, then cried some more.

The next day Jeanie was barely able to get her feet into her felt house slippers. When Gram saw her limping, she said, "I never should have let you go! Sit down and let me see."

When Jeanie took off one sock, Gram looked at the swollen foot and said, "You're going to be miserable for a few days, but they'll be all right—except for the chilblains."

"Chilblains?"

Gram nodded soberly. "You'll find out!" She sighed and shook her head. "Never should have let you go!"

Jeanie agreed. If only she had listened to Gram!

By the time school started she was able to wear shoes again, but she had learned what chilblains were. Every time her feet got cold, they would itch and hurt at the same time. Gram gave her corn starch to rub on them, but Jeanie couldn't feel much relief.

"We used to rub our feet with raw potato," Gram told her, "when we didn't have corn starch."

"You've had chilblains?"

"You bet I have! But that was because I had to drive the cows down to the river for water when Papa was in the lumber camp—not because I was out playing!"

That winter passed quickly for Jeanie. She didn't stay home many Saturday nights. Often they'd go to Abbotsford for hot beef sandwiches or go to a show or play Monopoly at someone's house.

Her friend Pearl had begun dating a boy called Bud, and now and then Jeanie and Kenny would double-date

with them. "Mutt and Jeff" people called Bud and
Kenny, because there was at least a foot difference in
their heights. The better Jeanie got to know Pearl,
whose brown eyes danced with mischief, the more she
liked her. Those evenings were full of laughter over
silly little spontaneous things. Jeanie longed to share
the fun with Gram . . . but how?

Emma felt at ease about Jeanie again. She didn't
mind not hearing all the silly little details of her
outings. Children's foolishness!

And having those tonsils out was wise, Emma was
sure. It was clear that Jeanie was lively and happy
once again. But what, she wondered, will she do next
year if Kenny goes away?

When Kenny invited Jeanie to go tobogganing
again in January, she hesitated. "Well . . . I guess so . . .
if it's not cold!" Her feet still hurt whenever they
became chilled.

"It'll be all right if it stays like this," Kenny said.
"Did you get your snow boots?"

"They came a few days ago," Jeanie answered,
watching the steady drips from a row of icicles on the
eaves of the school building. "I haven't worn them yet,
but that sheepskin lining looks like it will keep my feet
warm!"

Saturday morning, when Jeanie saw that the frost
flowers on her bedroom window had melted down to
the thick layer of ice at the bottom of the pane, she was
delighted. Her feet wouldn't freeze today! But as soon
as she got out of bed she felt a vague achiness. Instead
of getting dressed, she sat huddled by the oven door.

Gram came in from milking. "Haven't you eaten
yet? My goodness, you aren't even dressed! Aren't you
feeling well?"

Jeanie groaned. "I don't know what's wrong with me. I've never felt like this before."

Gram washed her hands and said, "Too bad Kenny's folks don't have a telephone. You could call and tell him not to come."

Jeanie, who was feeling worse by the minute, didn't even protest.

Kenny's grin faded as soon as he arrived. "Gee . . . what's wrong with you?"

She shrugged. "I don't know. I feel awful!"

After a few awkward moments, he said, "Well, I guess I'd better get back. Hope you feel better soon!"

Jeanie was still huddled by the oven door when Gram went to take her afternoon nap. All of a sudden she felt a "ping" on her leg—like she was being pricked by a sliver. She looked to see what it was, and there was a blister. While she was still looking at it, she found another one. She went to show Helen.

"Chicken pox!" Helen said with authority. "You mean you've never had it?"

Jeanie sorrowfully shook her head and staggered back to the oven door. She knew where she'd caught it—she'd stayed overnight with Grace just before her little brother broke out.

By the time Gram got up, blisters were popping out like popcorn. "Well, you can't stay upstairs in the cold," she said, feeling Jeanie's forehead. "Let's borrow Helen's cot and put it under the east window."

When Carl came to the door on Monday, he took one glance at her and burst out laughing. "I know it's not funny to you, but you sure are an awful sight!" He shook his head. "Just think . . . a few more years, and you might've got 'em from your kids!"

Wednesday's mail brought a letter from Kenny. It was written in pencil on glossy paper and was hard to read.

Dearest Jeanie,

*Grace told me you have the chicken pox!
Gee! That's awful. I hope you're feeling
better by now.*

*My Mom says don't scratch the ones on
your face. Don't get that pretty face messed
up!*

*Tobogganing was fun. What a slide! But
it would have been a lot more fun with you
there.*

*Take good care of yourself. I wish I could
do something to help.*

I love you!

                                        Kenny

There was a whole row of x's at the bottom.

Gram didn't ask to see the letter, and Jeanie didn't
offer to show it to her. She put it on the table where she
could reach it, and whenever Gram left the room,
Jeanie reread those precious words. For years she had
been afraid to dream that someone would actually
love her, and now someone really did—and a special
someone at that!

The days dragged by. Sometimes Helen came and
talked, but most of the time Gram kept the door closed
so Jeanie could rest. If only they had a radio!

On Friday there was another letter from Kenny,
who wrote that it was a good thing it wasn't prom time.

The prom! She hadn't even thought about it. Out
came the catalogs. After several days of planning, she
decided to take the bodice off last year's dress and use
the same skirt. She'd make a long torso top from a
darker pink moire taffeta and sew black velvet ribbons
down the front to tie in bows.

The next week Jeanie was peppered with scabs but
no longer feeling sick. She wished it were warm
enough to be upstairs. Even the little noises Gram made

irritated her—and her loud talking made Jeanie clench her jaws and plug her ears when Gram wasn't looking.

The day Jeanie went back to school, Grace had saved a seat on the bus for her. She squeezed Jeanie's hand, her eyes shining with excitement. "I couldn't wait for you to get back, so I could tell you in person. Myrtle's going to have a baby!"

Jeanie let out a squeal. "When?"

"The end of June or the first part of July."

"Oh, I wish they lived closer. Wouldn't it be fun to help Myrtle with the baby?"

Grace's smile vanished. "Who knows when I'll even see the baby? I want to start business school right after graduation."

Jeanie had only been back a few days when Pearl got bronchitis and was home for two weeks. It seemed like ages since they had had a good talk. When Pearl was finally feeling well again, she came home with Jeanie and stayed overnight. Cuddled deep under the warm covers, they talked and talked.

Between yawns Pearl said, "You and Kenny are different. You never fight!"

Jeanie laughed. "Maybe we don't fight like some couples do—call each other names or refuse to talk to each other—but we certainly disagree. I hate dance halls and taverns, and I wish he wouldn't go to those places. I don't even like wedding dances. I hate the noise and the smell of beer. I'm not used to anyone drinking—except my Uncle Hank, and I know how much trouble that's caused."

In church the first Sunday in March, Jeanie noticed Ruby's teary eyes and sad face. "What's the matter?" she whispered.

"I'll tell you later," Ruby whispered back.

Jeanie found it even harder than usual to concentrate on the service, and she shot anxious glances at

Ruby throughout. Afterward Ruby told her the news: Chet had been drafted! He was leaving for boot camp in a few days!

There had been no doubt for quite a while that Chet was the one for Ruby. Everybody liked the husky guy with the wide grin. And now he was being drafted. For a moment, as goose bumps raced along Jeanie's arms, she couldn't say a word. Whenever war was mentioned she felt chills, but now, for the first time, she actually knew someone who was going.

Finally she found her voice. "Oh, golly! Where will he be stationed?"

Ruby shook her head. "We don't know. He'll go to boot camp and then he'll be transferred somewhere for more training. I think I'll go to the city and work."

Jeanie stared at her long, straight lashes and the faint lines at the outside corners of her eyes that crinkled when she laughed. Oh, how she hurt for Ruby. There was no telling where Chet would be stationed or when they would see each other again. She hated to see her cousin go so far away, but she couldn't blame her if she wanted to go to Milwaukee or Chicago to work.

That day there were no giggles.

One morning in April, Kenny wasn't waiting when Jeanie got to school. A neighbor girl, Ruthie, said he had pneumonia.

Pneumonia! Jeanie felt icy fingers of fear clutch her stomach. She remembered when she was five and Roy had pneumonia. He had almost died. She couldn't keep from crying as she told Gram that night.

It was difficult to concentrate on schoolwork. Everyone she talked to asked how Kenny was, and she didn't know! Gram wouldn't let her go and see him. She didn't want Jeanie to catch it and, anyway, it wasn't proper for a girl to go and see a boy.

"This is different!" Jeanie pleaded, but Gram wouldn't relent. Jeanie had to content herself with sending notes with Ruthie.

When Ruthie told Jeanie that Kenny was really sad that she hadn't come to see him, she resolved to plead with Gram again. "But, Mama! I gotta go and see him— just a few minutes! I won't go real close to him!"

Reluctantly, Gram agreed that she could go.

Kenny was lying on a cot in the dining room near the oil heater, looking pale and coughing. After a few minutes he closed his eyes, and Jeanie didn't know what to do until his mother came downstairs.

"The doctor says he's better," said his mom, "but I don't see how he'll be able to go to the prom in two weeks."

Jeanie cried all the way back to school, but the kids pretended not to notice her swollen eyes. A tall skinny boy with a lot of pimples asked her to go to the prom with him if Kenny couldn't go.

"He'll be well by then," she told him with a confident toss of her head, but the picture of Kenny lying there not saying anything haunted her.

Oh, how Jeanie prayed for Kenny to get well. She hadn't prayed as earnestly since the day baby Rosalie was taken to the hospital. It wasn't the prom that was so important to her. She just wanted Kenny well again.

He was back in school, still pale and coughing a lot, two days before the prom, but he didn't laugh and tease.

"Hate to break our record," he said the first day he was back, "but I don't want you to get sick."

Jeanie knew what he was talking about. He had managed somehow to steal a quick kiss every school day that term.

She assured him she wasn't afraid, and they managed a longer-than usual kiss under a stairwell. "I missed you so much!" she whispered.

"That's how I felt when you had the chicken pox!" he whispered back, holding her close.

On Friday, the day of the prom, Jeanie brought her dress to school so she could change at Hank and Beulah's house. She'd left the bows untied because she didn't want to wrinkle the ribbon. When she did try to tie them that night, they turned this way and that . . . every way but the right way. Jeanie was nearly in tears by the time Beulah came to see how she was doing.

Out came needle and thread, and Beulah sewed the stubborn ribbons into place. Jeanie would have to rip her way out of the dress before she could sleep tonight!

They hadn't been at the prom long before Jeanie realized that Kenny was in no condition to be there. Long before the evening was over, they asked another couple for a ride home. In the car they held hands, and Jeanie longed to hold Kenny close. He didn't say a lot . . . he didn't have to.

"Spring is more welcome every year," Emma told Ella, who had come over to visit while Henry went to Ogema. They strolled around the yard looking for the first green sprouts.

Ella ignored her remark. "A few more weeks, and Grace will be graduating," she shouted in Emma's ear.

"What does she plan to do?"

They stopped walking while Ella told her of Grace's plan to go to business college in Duluth.

"That sounds good," Emma said. "That would be a good thing for Jeanie to do, but she says she doesn't want any part of office work and typing."

"At least we don't have to be concerned about their being drafted like the boys," Ella shouted.

Emma nodded. "I read the other day that over sixteen million men have already registered for the draft."

They were quiet a few moments, thinking of how the Germans had overrun most of Scandinavia and many countries of western Europe.

"I just hate to read the headlines lately," Emma continued. "What's going to have to happen before the Nazis are stopped?" She sighed. "I feel so sorry for the German people. Most of them can't be in favor of what's going on."

"That's always the way," Ella shouted. "The governments make the decisions, and the people do the suffering."

Later, over a cup of tea, Ella leaned close to Emma. "I've been thinking," she said. "I want to go to Lake Geneva to help Myrtle when the baby comes. Grace will be in Duluth by then. I'd like to have Jeanie come and keep house for the menfolk while I'm gone."

Emma frowned. "Oh . . . I don't know. . . . " She shook her head. "She hasn't done that much cooking—just for the two of us now and then. And she's such a giddy head."

Now it was Ella's turn to frown. "Ma! She's just a young girl—no different from my girls, except she hasn't had to do as much work. She'll learn! I'll show her how to do things. I trust her!"

"Hmmph! I'm glad you do! She sure doesn't take after her mother! I can't remember having to tell Emmie to do things over and over again."

"Well," Ella demanded, "is it all right if I ask her?"

Emma shrugged. "Go ahead." She shook her finger at Ella. "But don't come complaining to me if she doesn't do what she's supposed to! Land knows I try to teach her what I can, but her mind's off somewhere else."

The garden work was more difficult than ever for Emma that spring. Well, at seventy-two she couldn't expect to have the energy she had at forty. But the ground lay ready to work, and the flower beds needed attention. She would just do a little at a time.

Jeanie helped when she was home, but her weekends were full with spring activities. Emma was glad she had the opportunity to be with other young people.

So day after day, Emma would hoe a little and rest, hoe a little more and rest. It had always been her habit to finish one task before she began another, but if this was the only way to accomplish something, she'd have to change her habits.

At least I can get the peas in today, she told herself one day in early May. She had to rest three times before she finished hoeing a trench for the seeds. It made her dizzy to bend over and drop them in, so she had to straighten up several times before she finished. Covering the seeds was the easiest. She even sang as she worked, tamping the soil firm with a keen sense of satisfaction.

Out of breath, heart pounding, she walked slowly to the porch swing and sat down. She could see the deep, rich red-brown row from where she sat. Oh, it was a good feeling to see it planted. *Thank you, Lord!* she whispered. *Look at what the two of us did!*

Seven

It was a sunny but windy Sunday in June, and the young people from Jeanie's neighborhood had gathered at the Blombergs' house near Stone Lake to play volleyball. Jeanie went along, even though she disliked ball games of any kind. No matter how hard she tried, she was always a bit too early or a bit too late to make contact with the ball—not much of an asset to her team.

Consequently, no one paid any attention when she wandered off and sat on a bicycle instead of playing. She gazed at the clouds and thought about the long summer stretching out ahead. Myrtle's baby would be coming soon, and Jeanie thought about the job in store for herself—looking after Uncle Henry and the boys while Aunt Ella went to look after Myrtle. Aunt Ella assured her she would do fine, but Jeanie sensed that Gram wasn't so confident. Jeanie had a nagging fear that Gram was right.

Brrr. The breeze was cold. She wrapped her arms around herself and turned her back to the wind.

"Hey! You look cold!" said a voice behind her.

Jeanie turned and looked into a pair of lively, laughing brown eyes. A good-looking boy in a brown suede jacket extended his hand.

"I'm Eric."

"I'm Jeanie," she replied.

Smiling as though he knew a great deal more about her than she suspected, he said, "I know. Here, take my jacket. I was about to take it off anyway."

She shot him a grateful smile. "Thanks! I'm freezing!"

"Funny I haven't seen you before. I come up here a lot." He leaned back against a tree with his arms folded. He was considerably taller than Kenny.

"Where do you live?" she asked.

"Chicago. My folks have a summer home up here."

"Are you out of high school?" she asked, holding his jacket around her shoulders.

"I just graduated. How about you?"

"I'll be a senior in the fall."

"And then what?" he asked.

It was more a challenge than a question.

Jeanie shrugged. "I don't know. What about you?"

Eric sat down cross-legged with his back against the tree. He planned to go to college in the fall, he told her. He loved airplanes and wanted to be a pilot.

All the while he talked, his eyes never left hers, and she found herself beginning to feel a bit uncomfortable.

"I want to travel—a lot, " he concluded. "Maybe I'll enlist in the Air Corps."

It was Eric's strong features that hovered in Jeanie's mind that night, not Kenny's. For almost three years no one else had caught her attention, but now. . . . She rolled over and told herself he would go back to the city and she probably wouldn't see him again, but deep in her heart she hoped she would. There was something mysterious about this boy. She couldn't decide if he was laughing with her or amused by her. And she liked his direct way of speaking and the way he held her eyes—even if it did scare her a little. He knew a world that was completely strange to her, and she wanted to know more about it—much more.

Monday afternoon Helen and Roy went to Tomahawk. As soon as the car was out of the driveway, Jeanie hitched the wooden rocker next to Gram's. Gram put down her knitting.

"I met a real nice boy Sunday at the volleyball game. I wanted to tell you about him when I got home, but I didn't want anyone else to know." She shrugged. "Maybe I won't even see him again. He lives in Chicago."

Gram nodded and waited for Jeanie to continue.

"His name is Eric Benson. He's different from the boys around here. His parents have a summer home up here."

"I've heard of the Bensons. They seem like a nice family. They have relatives here." Family background meant a lot to Gram.

"I'd really like to see him again—but I feel like I'm two-timing Kenny."

Gram nodded and thought a moment. "I can understand why you'd feel that way. But at your age you should have other friends. You're awfully young to be going with only one boy." She leaned forward and shook her finger at Jeanie. "But I sure don't want you running around with every Tom, Dick, and Harry!"

Jeanie went to Roy and Helen's living room to play the piano, as she often did when everyone else was gone, leaving Emma to sit and think. Life was so complicated. She had been wondering whether she should let Jeanie go out alone with Kenny, or insist that they double-date, and wondering how late she should allow her to stay out. Now there was this Eric—a city boy—to worry about. There were times Emma felt it was more difficult to bring up Jeanie than it had been to raise all thirteen of her own. Of course Papa had been there to allay her fears and give good counsel.

She sighed and picked up her knitting. *Maybe Jeanie won't even see him again. No sense worrying about it. After all, being from the city doesn't necessarily make him a bad boy.*

Wednesday evening about seven, Helen poked her head in the door, smiling broadly. "Jeanie! There's someone here to see you," she said, sounding pleased.

Jeanie followed her through the house and out the back door. There stood Eric beside his bicycle, talking to Roy.

He flashed a smile at her and said, a bit self-consciously, "It was such a nice evening, I thought I'd take a ride. Are you busy?"

"No . . . uh, no!" Jeanie stammered. "Come and meet my grandmother." *Can this really be happening?* she thought. *Eric, right here in this house! Good thing I told Gram about him.*

As Eric followed her through the house, she explained that her grandmother was very hard of hearing. When she introduced him, Gram smiled pleasantly and asked if he would be here all summer.

In a few well-chosen words, spoken loudly enough to set the ceiling light fixture quivering, he told her he would be in Chicago part of the time. He added that he liked being in Wisconsin better than in the city.

Gram smiled at that.

"Want to walk down to the bridge?" Jeanie asked, at a loss to know what to do.

"Fine with me," Eric said, smiling down at her.

"We're going to walk down to the bridge," she shouted in Gram's ear.

"Be back before dark," Gram ordered.

Still overwhelmed by Eric's actually coming to see her, Jeanie struggled to start a conversation. "How far away do you live—I mean, where is your summer home?" she asked as they trudged down the hill.

"Oh, about three miles, I guess. It didn't seem far. Do you like to ride bikes?"

Jeanie laughed nervously. "I don't have a bike, but I've ridden other kids'. I'm not very strong." She gestured toward the west. "I've never been able to get to the top of that hill."

He didn't reply, but Jeanie could feel his eyes on her. At the bridge they leaned over the wide concrete railing and talked. Then Eric patted it and said, "Let's sit up here."

Before she could answer, he had grasped her waist and swung her up onto the concrete railing.

"You're strong!" she said, a bit startled.

He shrugged. "You aren't very heavy."

He hitched himself up beside her and put his arm protectively behind her.

"Tell me more about Chicago," Jeanie said, feeling a bit more calm.

"Well . . . the downtown section is on the lake shore. It's called 'The Loop' because the elevated trains make a loop."

"Elevated trains? Trains like the ones that come through Ogema?"

Eric chuckled. "Not quite!"

Jeanie listened with interest as he talked about the train stations, Midway Airport, and Grant Park. What would they talk about next?

"Listen to the frogs singing!" she said.

Eric laughed. "Frogs croak, they don't sing!"

"Yes, they do," she insisted.

"If you say so," he said indulgently. He swatted a mosquito on his forehead.

She killed a mosquito on her arm. "I think they've found us. Maybe we'd better go back."

As they strolled up the hill, Eric reached for her hand. It was time, she decided, to let Eric know about Kenny.

"I've been going with a boy from Rib Lake since I was a freshman," she blurted out.

"I know that," Eric said calmly.

"And you still came to see me?"

He squeezed her hand. "You bet. You're too young to be going with only one guy."

They walked around the house to where his bicycle was parked under the box elder tree by the garage. He gave her hand another little squeeze before he let go. His gaze burned through the dusky blue light, saying a great deal more than he put into words. "Is it all right if I come over again next Wednesday evening?"

Not wanting to appear too eager, Jeanie gave a nonchalant shrug. "Fine! See you then."

The gravel scrunched as he sped away.

The hour that flew by for Jeanie simply dragged for Emma. She tried not to keep going to the window to look down at the bridge, but found herself doing it anyway. Too restless to sit and knit, she decided to go and find a few chips for starting the fire in the morning. She stopped to talk with Helen, who was sitting at her kitchen table reading the *Journal*.

"Have you seen this boy before?" Emma asked.

"Oh, yes. The Bensons are a real nice family. They have a summer home near my sister Lily's."

Emma shook her head. "I don't know . . . these city boys. . . ."

"What's wrong with 'city boys'?" Helen challenged. "Jeanie needs to broaden her world. What do you want her to do? Marry that little Kenny and live in a company house in Rib Lake while he works in the mill?"

"Oh forgoodnessakes! They're just little kids!" Emma hustled out for her chips. No use getting into an argument with Helen; it was plain where she stood. After all, Eric was Swedish, like Helen.

As she picked up chips, Emma chuckled at herself. Why shouldn't that please Helen? Wasn't Emma herself more comfortable with Kenny because his family was German?

As planned, Kenny came out in his parents' royal blue Pontiac on Friday night to take Jeanie to the show in Rib Lake. On the way home she said, as casually as she could, "A boy from Chicago who has a summer home here rode his bike over to see me Wednesday night. I met him at a volleyball game last Sunday."

Kenny kept his eyes on the road. "Well, it's a free world," he said. "I guess I can't stop him." He turned the conversation back to his summer job with Herman Schmidt, a plumber. "I'm learning a lot," he said, "but most of the time I just dig holes. Boy! That clay can be like concrete!"

Jeanie looked forward to the moment when he'd park by the east end of the house, turn off the ignition, and lean over and gather her in his arms. Oh, those kisses! They no longer stopped at one or two.

But later that night as Jeanie crawled into bed, she felt sick and confused. Kenny had begun to talk about going to Chicago in the fall if Ray, who had gone several months ago, could find a job for him. It would be bad enough just facing school without him, but what would she do if he went away?

And, in another corner of her mind, a little voice whispered, "If Kenny is that important to you, why are you thinking so much about Eric?"

On Tuesday Jeanie went to Aunt Ella's to "learn the ropes."

"Now, you'll have to keep your head on and remember everything she tells you!" Gram warned as Jeanie got ready to leave.

"It sure would help if she had confidence in me," Jeanie grumbled as she hiked along. "She doesn't think I can do anything right!"

Aunt Ella gave her a tour from cellar to upstairs and showed her how she did her work. When they had finished, they sat down at the long table for a cup of tea and peanut butter cookies. It made Jeanie feel positively grown up to have tea with Aunt Ella.

"You know," she said, reaching for a cookie, "this is the first time you and I ever had a chance to talk alone."

Aunt Ella looked a bit surprised. "Why, come to think of it, you're right. There always has been someone else around." Her eyes twinkled, and she said in a confidential tone, "It's nice, isn't it?"

"I bet you miss the girls," Jeanie said thoughtfully.

"Oh, my land! Do I ever. The guys aren't much company. If they aren't reading the paper or listening to the radio, they're talking about work or ball games. Oh, I forgot to tell you—when you get caught up a little in the afternoon, you can turn the radio on for a while."

Batteries wore out fast, and you didn't turn the radio on if you weren't able to pay attention to it.

"Now, let's see . . . have I forgotten to tell you anything?"

She smiled, and Jeanie wondered if Gram's cheeks had been as round and smooth as rolls rising on the counter when she was Aunt Ella's age.

"I'm warning you, Jeanie, you'll get tired of peeling potatoes. Fried potatoes for breakfast and supper, boiled potatoes for dinner." She took a sip of tea and chuckled. "When I was a girl, I told myself I would never feed my family fried potatoes because I had already peeled and fried so many. But here I am doing just what Ma did—cooking what we have on hand!"

Jeanie finished her last bite of cookie and sighed. "I hope I do everything right."

"You will," Aunt Ella said. "I'm not worried."

"Gram sure is." Jeanie traced a yellow flower on the oilcloth with the tip of the spoon handle. "She doesn't think I can do anything right!"

"I guess I felt the same way about my girls, until I saw what they could do when I wasn't around."

Jeanie's head snapped up. "You did?"

Aunt Ella nodded. "Oh, yes. We mothers see our kids forgetting things and being giddy-headed, and we don't realize that they'll settle down and do what they should when they're on their own."

Jeanie's eyes went back to the flower. "I just wish Gram wouldn't scold all the time. I don't even get in the door at night before she says, 'Now, go put an apron on!'"

Aunt Ella threw back her head and laughed, then stopped short at the hurt expression on Jeanie's face. "Oh, Jeanie, I'm sorry! It just struck me funny because she always said that to me when I was a girl!"

"She did? I thought—"

Aunt Ella interrupted her with a wave. "Don't let it bother you. It's just her way!"

Jeanie could feel tears welling up. "I try, but sometimes I just want to run away. I know that every time I touch something, she's going to tell me that I'm doing it wrong."

Aunt Ella glanced at the clock, pushed back her chair, and gave Jeanie a quick hug. "Well, now's your chance to show her what you can do right!"

It was just a few days later that Aunt Ella called to say that little Hazel Ellen had been born. She would wait until Myrtle was ready to come home from the hospital before she took the bus to Lake Geneva.

The day Ella was leaving, she showed Jeanie what she had started for dinner. "There's plenty of bread for tomorrow, but you'll need to bake on Wednesday. I'll tell Uncle Henry to bring home some hamburger when he takes me to the bus, and you can make meat loaf for dinner tomorrow and a casserole the next day. I don't ever keep fresh meat more than two days in summer, even though the cellar seems cool."

As soon as the dinner dishes were washed and everyone had gone, Jeanie perched on the high green stool and planned menus. She flipped through the recipe cards Aunt Ella had left on the counter—salmon loaf, meat loaf, corn casserole.

The next morning, with one eye on the clock, Jeanie filled the coffeepot, put potatoes in a pan to fry, brought up milk and eggs from the cellar, and set the table. By the time she heard the men coming in from milking, breakfast was ready.

They ate heartily and went back to work. After they had gone, she sat quietly for a few moments, a bit dazed. She wasn't accustomed to moving so fast as soon as she got up.

"It'll get over ninety again," Uncle Henry had said. To Jeanie it felt like ninety degrees already. She combed her damp hair away from her face and secured a troublesome lock with a bobby pin.

I'm glad I don't have to bake bread today, she thought. Aunt Ella had advised her to get the bread started early when the weather was hot, so she could allow the fire to go out a while in the afternoon.

Jeanie had expected to feel a sense of freedom without Gram or anyone else telling her what to do. For a few days, this domestic realm was hers to rule. She had planned to arrange wild flowers to give touches of color here and there. She would keep the house, and herself, as attractive as possible.

But by the time she had washed the dinner dishes and swept the kitchen, she just wanted to collapse on the living room sofa. At five o'clock another meal must be on the table, and she wondered how she'd find the energy to make all those trips up and down the cellar stairs. Did Aunt Ella's legs feel drained of energy each time she climbed those stairs? Did she lean against the door frame a moment until the darkness went away?

The next day, after a good night's sleep, Jeanie's enthusiasm returned. Instead of slapping plates on the table as they came from the stack, Jeanie picked out only the yellow ones. They looked pretty with the yellow and green flowered oilcloth. When she had her own home, she would never set a table with all sorts of odd dishes.

Now to bake the bread! Gram had allowed her to bake bread several times, and she felt confident. Even though her arms were aching by the time she plopped the kneaded dough into a huge bowl to rise, it felt good to see it look just like Aunt Ella's.

Sitting on the stool peeling potatoes again, Jeanie understood what Aunt Ella meant. If Aunt Ella had a penny for every potato she had peeled, she'd surely be a millionaire.

At dinner time the fragrance of baking bread filled the house, and she was glad she had heeded Aunt Ella's suggestion to bake a pan of rolls so the men could have them for dinner.

Harvey buttered one and said, "Remember how Edward would always get you giggling when you and Gram ate with us?"

"Do I ever!" Jeanie exclaimed. "All he had to say was, 'Jeanie! Tee-hee-hee!' and I'd start."

"Yeah, and Gramma would frown at you and say, 'Now, that's enough!' but by that time everyone was laughing."

When they had eaten and gone outside, Jeanie spread the one remaining roll with butter. It was delicious. If Gram could only see her now!

If she started the fire at three-thirty, she calculated, she could have supper ready by five.

As soon as she had finished washing dishes, she turned on the radio and swept the floor to the strains of "Deep Purple." She dusted the living room as Glen Miller's orchestra played "Lilacs in the Rain."

This was living! If only the REA would come through soon, so she could get a radio! "This year, for sure!" Roy had said.

There was time for a bit of rest after the house was in order, so she relaxed on the sofa while Tommy Dorsey's orchestra played "Stardust."

The clock struck three leaden bongs, and Jeanie woke with a start and jumped up so suddenly her head spun. She needed to get more little potatoes to boil in their jackets for tomorrow and start the fire. She crumpled newspaper in the firebox, added slim sticks of kindling, struck a match, and watched the flames spread. Then she added sticks of wood and went to get the potatoes.

Back in the kitchen, she couldn't hear the fire crackle. No . . . the wood was just as she had put it in. Hastily she crumpled more paper, added more kindling, and lit it.

When she finished taking sprouts off and washing the potatoes, she checked the fire again. "Oh, no!" she wailed. Again the paper and kindling had burned, but the wood was merely blackened.

Four o'clock. Jeanie took out two pieces of wood and added more paper and kindling. By now her knees were feeling shaky. Gram was right—she couldn't do anything right. She'd never have supper ready on time.

When that attempt failed, she ran out to the woodshed, found a few sticks of dry wood in a far corner, and ran back in. It was almost four-thirty, and she hadn't even peeled the potatoes she had boiled yesterday.

When Uncle Henry came in and dried his hands on the roller towel, Jeanie said, "I had trouble starting the fire, so supper isn't quite ready. I'm sorry!" She knew they were hungry and eager to get done with milking.

Uncle Henry glanced at the partly-set table. "Call when it's ready," he said gruffly, and took the newspaper to the living room. He didn't sound angry, but she knew he wasn't happy.

It was almost five-thirty when she called them, and she didn't have to call twice. Harvey and Jim slid along the bench to their places and began dishing up their plates before Uncle Henry had put down his paper.

Through the following days, Jeanie managed to keep the fire burning. She did spill the only remaining milk one evening, and burned a pan of oatmeal cookies, and made lumpy gravy.

When Uncle Henry went to pick Aunt Ella up at the bus stop a week later, Jeanie was more than ready to go home.

"Uncle Henry told me you did a real good job," Aunt Ella said when she got home and they sat down for a cup of tea. She smiled. "I don't suppose he told you that!"

Jeanie shook her head. "I really didn't expect him to."

"Wise girl. Men just take things for granted—until they have to do it themselves."

"Doesn't that bother you?" Jeanie asked.

"Oh, it did—a long while ago. Now I just go about my work and don't look for appreciation. The Bible says we're supposed to do everything 'as unto the Lord.' If we do that, we won't ever be disappointed."

Jeanie filed that idea away in the "things to think about later" section of her mind. "Tell me about the baby!" she urged.

Aunt Ella beamed. "Oh, she's just a little dolly— dark hair and dimples. I think she looks a lot like Harry. I just wish they didn't live so far away."

"I can't wait to see her!" Jeanie said. Other cousins had had babies before, of course, but Myrtle's was special.

Back at home, Jeanie didn't tell Gram about the problems she'd had. She did make certain to tell her what Uncle Henry had said to Aunt Ella.

Gram heaved a sigh of relief. "I'm glad," she said. "It was good experience for you."

The next Wednesday evening, Eric drove over with his father's car. He and Jeanie sat on the porch swing a while, then Eric said, "I brought a whole bunch of pictures with me. Come out to the car and see."

He turned the dome light on and sat with his cheek almost touching hers as he explained picture after picture. So this was Chicago!

When he left, Gram was waiting for Jeanie with a face like a thundercloud. "Young lady, I was about to come out and yank you out of that car! Don't you know better than to sit around with a boy in a car like that?"

Jeanie was so stunned she couldn't think of a thing to say. Eric had bestowed one gentle kiss when he left. Did Gram think—? She stifled the urge to laugh. Poor Eric! He was such a gentleman, and Gram thought he was a fast guy.

"Oh, Mama! We didn't do anything wrong!"

"Don't you get sassy, young lady! I saw you sitting with your heads so close it looked like one head!"

Jeanie shook her head and groaned. She pulled the rocker close to Gram and shouted in her ear. "Remember after the prom when we stayed out all night, and you told me not to feel bad as long as I knew I hadn't done anything wrong?"

Gram frowned, thought a moment, then nodded.

"Well, that's the way I feel now. You can't make me feel guilty," she said angrily, "because we didn't do anything wrong. We were looking at pictures!"

Gram gave her a that's-what-they-all-say look.

Jeanie got up and gave the chair a shove. What was the use trying to reason? Gram had her mind made up! She stomped to her room.

Emma was all smiles when Kenny and his folks came Sunday afternoon and invited Jeanie to go with them to a cousin's birthday party. But when the car was out of sight, self-pitying thoughts attacked her like a swarm of hornets.

Swinging gently on the porch swing, she fought those thoughts the best way she knew—with prayer. *Father, here I am, alone again. Seems like the older I get, the more I find myself alone. But the older I get, the closer You seem, so I'll just spend this nice afternoon with You.*

I do thank You for helping Jeanie when she was at Ella's. I was so afraid she'd have a terrible time, but they say she did real well.

She couldn't hear the swing squeak anymore, but she remembered how it sounded. Sparrows were probably chirping, and maybe the little wren was singing in the honeysuckle bush. She had seen it fly over there.

She couldn't hear herself sing anymore, either, but she sang regardless. "I need Thee every hour. . . ." It wasn't her own voice she heard in her memory, but Emmie's sweet singing. *My goodness! She'd be almost thirty-seven now. Can she see what's going on down here? Can she watch Jeanie grow up? What would she have done about Jeanie sitting out in the car with that young man?*

Emma sighed. Maybe she had misjudged them. They did have the dome light on.

One more school term—and then what? Nearly all the young girls went to the city unless they married a local boy. She sang a long while. "Draw me nearer, nearer blessed Lord. . . ." "Rock of Ages, cleft for me. . . . " "Just as I am without one plea, but that Thy blood was shed for me. . . . "

When she got hungry she went in and reheated some coffee and made a cheese sandwich. Sitting at the table, loneliness swept over her again as she looked up at Al's picture. There was so much she longed to share with him . . . ask him. Was she being too hard on Jeanie? too easy-going? If there was one thing she was determined to do, it was to keep that girl from getting proud and haughty. And, of course, see that she conducted herself like a proper young lady.

Tears came to Emma's eyes as she thought of how much she loved that girl. There were times she just wanted to hug her like a little tot, but of course she couldn't do that.

There were times, too, when she watched Jeanie's lithe young body, her shining hair flying in the wind, her gray-blue eyes sparkling with excitement, that she wanted to say, "Do you know how pretty you are?" But that would never do.

Oh, if only Emmie were alive! They could talk about Jeanie, laugh and enjoy her together.

Abruptly, she brushed crumbs from the table into her hand and put them on the porch railing for the birds. Enough of that "if only" thinking!

But she couldn't help one more thought: *if only I could be sure I'm doing what's right for Jeanie.*

The smell of new wood set Emma's pioneer blood stirring—and there was certainly plenty of new wood around Carl and Olga's place these days. Carl had been in the process of building a new house for months— doing it gradually, because his farm work had to be done right along with the building.

"We'll be in it before the baby comes in August," Carl had said in the spring, but on this July day, as Emma walked through the unfinished house, it looked as though the move would be made quite a while after the baby's arrival.

"We've managed so far," Olga said cheerfully. "We'll manage a few weeks more."

Using her apron as a basket, Emma picked up scraps of lumber around the building site for starting fires. Little Marvin tugged at her skirt and motioned for her to come with him.

"Yes! Yes! I'll come!" Emma assured him. "First I want to take this to the wood box."

He shook his head violently and pulled harder.

"Well, all right," she said and followed him, wood scraps and all, to a shady spot at the edge of the yard.

"Oh, my goodness! Will you look at that!" she exclaimed as she bent over for a closer look at the "town" the three children had built of wood scraps. "You want these, too?"

Three heads nodded.

"Well, I suppose so." She dropped her apron, and the wood scraps rolled out.

At least all the scraps are in one place, she reasoned. *I'll see if I can get the children to pick up more, so the scraps will be out of the men's way. Eventually they'll have to go to the wood box.*

"Tell you what," she said, spying a cardboard box. "If you find a piece of rope, I'll tie it on this box, and you can haul wood to your city."

They exchanged glances and grinned. Albert ran off to find a piece of rope, and Emma went to get a knife to make holes.

In the little log house, Jeanie was jabbering a steady stream to Olga as she set the table for dinner. "Do you think it's wrong for me to see two boys at the same time? It's not like I'm being deceptive," she added hastily. "They know I'm seeing both of them."

Olga put a stick of wood into the stove. "Eventually you'll have to stop seeing one of them—or both, if another boy comes into your life. Eventually someone is going to be hurt."

Jeanie held the bundle of silverware and stared out the window. "I guess I hadn't thought about that. I've just been having fun."

Olga picked up a fat loaf of bread and began to slice it. "I agree with Helen that you are too young to be tied down to one boy—but you need to be sure you don't allow either of them to build false hopes."

Before Jeanie could answer, Gram came in for a knife, her eyes sparkling, and told Olga about the children's block "city."

Olga chuckled as the screen door slammed behind Gram. "She's really in her glory today. How she enjoys seeing her children make progress." She turned from the stove, wooden spoon in hand. "She's about the most contented person I've ever met."

Jeanie thought about Olga's words that evening as she pumped a pail of water. Jeanie admired go-getters—people who wanted to do something great, made plans, set goals and achieved them—not people who were content with things just the way they were.

Sometimes when Gram sang as she went about her daily tasks, with that serene all's-right-with-the-world look on her face, Jeanie felt disgusted. *How can she be so happy? How can she be content to be home day after day, doing the same old things?*

And this was what Olga admired? She carried the water pail through the house, trying not to spill water on Helen's kitchen floor, and set it down on the bench with a thump.

Gram was sitting in her rocker braiding her long gray hair, as she did each night before she went to bed. Her face was radiant with a wasn't-this-a-wonderful-day expression.

"I can just see Carl's family in that new house," she said. "Olga won't know what to do with all the space! But I've never heard her complain about the old house."

Jeanie nodded. No need to shout a reply. As she undressed for bed, it was like a piece of puzzle fell into place. Gram delighted in progress and change when it was for someone else. But in her own life, she saw that any desire for change could bring hardship to others, so she chose to be content with things as they were.

Hmmm . . . when you thought of it that way, her contentment was an admirable quality. "I don't deserve her," Jeanie told her reflection. "She's absolutely unselfish! And you—" she shook her hairbrush at her image, "are a selfish beast."

Eight

Berry picking and sewing kept Jeanie busy through August—as well as spending time with Eric and Kenny.

One Wednesday evening, Eric left after a pleasant time together. Just as Jeanie was about to suds her face, there was a knock on the door. There stood Eric, looking embarrassed.

"I can't find my bike!" he whispered, forgetting that Gram wouldn't hear him even if he spoke aloud.

"Wait. I'll get a flashlight," Jeanie said.

Beaming the light ahead of them, they searched all around the yard. "Roy must have hidden it," Jeanie said. "It can't be far."

When they found it on the south side of the garage, Jeanie said, "I think he likes you. He wouldn't bother to do that if he didn't."

Eric pressed his cheek against Jeanie's. "I hope he's not the only one who likes me," he said wistfully.

Lying in bed, Jeanie thought about his words and then remembered what Olga had said. "Eventually someone is going to be hurt."

Who would the someone be? Kenny or Eric? She didn't want to hurt either of them. Why did things always have to get complicated?

The next day Jeanie sat on the porch swing hemming a skirt and comparing the "men in her life." Eric was more intelligent and had plans. Kenny said little about the future except that, the way Hitler was moving, he would probably be called into service soon. Eric was handsome; Kenny was cute. Eric was tall; it didn't appear that Kenny would even be as tall as Jeanie. Eric would probably never drink, but Kenny's family, like many German people, kept beer in the house.

Jeanie sighed. She finished hemming her skirt and abandoned her comparisons. The more she thought about the two boys' qualities, the more confused she felt.

"My brother can get me a job in Chicago," Kenny told Jeanie when he came to see her Saturday night.

Even though she had suspected that Kenny would eventually go to the city, his words left her weak. Attempting to keep her voice steady, she said, "Do you want to go to Chicago?"

Kenny took a firmer grip on her hand as they strolled in the twilight. "I don't want to leave you . . . but what is there to do around here? I always figured I'd go to the city sometime. I don't want to be a farmer or work in the mill."

"When will you go?"

"In about three weeks. I'll take the train from Merrill on September seventh."

"Three weeks!"

"Yeah. My mother's going to ship my clothes so I don't have to bother with luggage, and Ray'll meet me at Union Station. Man! He's been writing about all the places he's been. It sure sounds like fun. I've never been in a big city."

How can he sound so excited! He isn't even thinking about me back here at home!

Jeanie managed another question as the lump in her throat continued to grow. "Where will you live?"

"Guess we'll be at Vi and Art's a few weeks; then we plan to get a room at the YMCA."

Jeanie couldn't respond.

"The guys and I have been planning a little party the night before I leave—just you and me and Pete and Curly and Spike. Maybe Spike'll decide to bring a girl. We'll go out to the Blue Royal for chicken, and then Pete's folks said we can go out to their cottage at Harper's Lake."

Jeanie was thinking that she'd much rather spend that evening alone with Kenny.

"You sure are quiet," he said when they were sitting on the porch swing.

Jeanie want to tell him how empty her world would be without him, but instead she started to cry.

He held her close while she sobbed. "I'm going to miss you a lot. You know that! I'll come home for Christmas. And maybe I can find a job for you, so you can come down after you graduate."

That night Jeanie gently bumped Gram's bed and kissed her goodnight. She didn't try to tell her about Kenny leaving. She would have to speak too loud and anyway, she had a lot more crying to do before she could talk about it.

The day school started, Jeanie didn't even want to get up. It would be so different, so lonely without Grace . . . without Kenny. Thank goodness Pearl would still be there. Time and again that first day, Jeanie expected to see Kenny pop around a corner.

All too soon it was Saturday, September sixth . . . the day of Kenny's farewell party. Jeanie was ready long before seven, when Kenny had said he would be there. She paced from Gram's bedroom window to the east window, combed her hair again, and paced some more.

"Oh, forgoodnessakes, sit down!" Gram scolded. "You make me nervous."

Jeanie tried to read, but soon she was up peering out of the window again. It wasn't like Kenny to be late.

"You might just as well settle down," Gram said. "He's not going to come."

"Of course he's coming!" Jeanie shouted, her cheeks flushing with anger. How could Gram say such a thing? This was the last time they'd be together for months!

"Here he comes now!" she shouted triumphantly, spying the car. She gathered up her handbag and the shaving lotion and cologne set she had wrapped for a going-away gift.

Gram went to meet him. "I'll be in bed when you get back, son, so I'll say goodbye now. I hope you like your job and that everything goes well for you."

He held out his hand and nodded and smiled.

Impulsively, Gram reached out and hugged him. Gram, who never hugged anyone but little kids and relatives she hadn't seen for years! She waved from the east window as they drove off and again from the north window when they were out on the road. When Jeanie looked back, she saw her silhouetted in the west window.

Jeanie snuggled closer to Kenny. She planned to make the most of every moment of the evening.

When Kenny's car disappeared over the crest of the hill, Emma took off her glasses and dried her eyes. She would miss that boy.

With a sigh she sat down and began to knit. Jeanie's angry face appeared in her mind's eye. Why on earth did I say that he wasn't coming? Because I wished he wouldn't? Why do I feel so uneasy? Somehow I just didn't want them to go tonight.

Later, sitting on the edge of the bed in her nightgown, Emma prayed for a long while for Jeanie and Kenny—for their safety, for his trip on Sunday, for Jeanie's adjustment to having him gone.

She slept soundly until eleven-thirty. Although she hadn't told Jeanie to be home at a specific time, midnight was considered her time to be in. Each time Emma saw car lights, she thought, *Here they come*. But time after time the car went past.

At twelve-thirty she began to get a bit tense. She peered out of the window. It was raining . . . not hard, but enough to make the roads slippery.

At one o'clock she was too restless to stay in bed. She walked around the house, saw another car go past, prayed for peace, and went back to bed.

She must have slept, she realized, because it was almost two when she looked at the clock again. Oh, those kids! Where on earth were they! Even though it was Kenny's last night home, they had no business being out this late.

She dozed. Struggling out of a confusing dream, Emma opened her eyes. Nearly three-fifteen! An icy shaft of fear plunged deep into the center of her being. For a moment she was unable to move. She got out of bed, slipped on her robe, and paced from window to window trying to stop trembling. *I knew it! I just felt like something was going to happen*. But surely, if there had been an accident, someone would have called.

She sat down in her rocker, hands and jaws clenched. In her mind's eye she could see a big old white house— Taylor's Funeral Home.

She struggled to her feet. *No! I won't allow myself to think such thoughts! Oh, Father! Help me!*

Pacing around the house, she tried to recall comforting Scripture. "Thou wilt keep him in perfect peace whose mind is stayed on Thee: because he trusteth in Thee." *Oh, I want to trust you, Lord. You love those children perfectly. You will care for them.*

"Be careful for nothing: but in everything by prayer and supplication with thanksgiving, let your requests be made known unto God." She repeated the words in a whisper.

Twisted, battered metal, shattered glass . . . still young bodies. *No! No! No! I will not think about that!*

Maybe if she turned on the light, those images would leave. Wearily, Emma sat down again and tried to knit. Her hands trembled so badly she dropped stitches. She laid her knitting aside.

Maybe they were parked in the car somewhere! A different fear plunged its icy shaft into her again. A memory almost eighteen years old made her catch her breath—Emmie on her knees, sobbing in Emma's lap. "Oh, Mama! It was just that one time!"

Oh, no! Not that! Almost four-thirty now. What would she say to them when they came? Demand an explanation? On her feet again, Emma turned off the light and wandered from one window to the other on shaky legs. *Jesus! Jesus! If anything happens to that girl, I don't think I can stand it. Oh, please Lord, let everything be all right!*

Laughing and teasing after they finished dinner, Jeanie, Kenny, and their friends headed back to the car.

"I didn't know it was going to rain! Oh, my poor hair!" Jeanie wailed as she ran with her handbag protecting her head.

On the way to the cottage, just before Niggeman's curve, Pete said, "Take 'er easy on that curve. My brother rolled over there two weeks ago."

"Yeah, I know," Kenny said, slowing down and taking a firmer grip on the wheel. "It's like driving on lard."

The words had hardly left his mouth when there was a startling scrunch of gravel. Then they were rolling and bumping for what seemed to be a very long time. Then silence . . . darkness.

"Ken! Turn off the ignition," Spike yelled.

"I can't find it! Oh, my gosh. Is everyone all right?"

Pete yelled, "Curly's face is bleeding all over! We've gotta get her outta here!"

"Jeanie! Are you all right?" came Kenny's anguished voice.

She was lying on something hard, but she found she could move her arms and legs. She tried to lift her head. "My hair's caught in something!"

"Just take it easy," Kenny said breathlessly. "We gotta flag down a car and get Curly to the doctor."

Car lights! "Here, let's get her out."

Jeanie heard a car slow down and stop. A man growled, "What! I'm not gettin' my car all messed up!"

Tires squealed as he roared off, leaving them standing with the bleeding girl.

In the glare of the headlights, Jeanie had been able to see the grass coming through the shattered windshield on her right. Her hair was caught in the door.

Spike was still in the car. "Gotta get you outta here!' he said, and tried to pull her hair out of the door. It wouldn't move.

More car lights. Voices yelling. A car stopped a moment and then sped away with Pete and Curly.

More lights. People. Kenny's frantic voice. "Her hair is caught! We gotta get her out. This thing could catch on fire!"

"Give me a knife, somebody," Spike yelled. "I'll cut her hair off."

"No!" someone else said. "We can lift it. One. Two. Three. Heave!"

Jeanie pulled her hair out, turned over on her knees, and crawled out of the window and up a gravel-covered slope, where she collapsed into Kenny's arms.

There were more cars stopping, more people. Kenny led her across the highway away from the crowd.

He was shaking, crying. "Curly's all cut up, and it's my fault!"

Jeanie held him close.

Then they were being ushered into the car of a neighbor Kenny knew. "How you kids ever got out of that thing alive. . . ." He shook his head. "I'll take you to Doc Baker's. You better have him check all of you over."

The doctor was stitching Curly's face when they arrived, and they had to wait behind the closed door. Kenny went from one to the other. "You sure you're all right?"

Jeanie let out a cry when she saw Kenny's left arm. Blood had soaked through his gold sweater near the wrist. "Feels like there's a piece of glass in it," he said when he pulled the cuff up.

The door opened, and the doctor guided a pale Curly to a chair. A bandage covered her left eyebrow.

"It's not bad." Doc Baker said. "She has a cut under the eyebrow. I'd like to see her Monday. She'll probably have quite a bruise, too."

Kenny sagged into a chair. "I thought her whole face was cut up when I saw all that blood."

The doctor checked them over, removed a piece of glass from Kenny's arm, and shook his head. "I hope you know how fortunate you all are!"

Jeanie asked if she could use the phone.

"Roy! It's Jeanie!" She struggled to keep from crying. "We had an accident. We're all right, except one girl got a cut. I'll be at Kenny's house."

Roy said they'd come just as soon as he did the milking next morning. Jeanie assumed he would tell Gram, who would surely worry if she weren't home by midnight. It was already after eleven.

The neighbor drove Curly home and then drove the others back out to the wreck. Lying in its top, the car didn't look two feet high.

Jeanie felt an arm around her shoulders. It was Hank—white-faced and shaking. "I was at Kelly's when someone came in and said you kids had rolled over. When I saw that car, I thought no one coulda got out of that alive." He offered to drive her home, but she told him about the phone call to Roy.

At Kenny's house, his father shuffled around the house mumbling in a deep voice. He was glad no one had been badly injured, but he was plenty upset about his nice Pontiac.

Kenny's mother took Jeanie upstairs and got her settled in what had been Elvira's bed. After what seemed like just a few minutes of terrifying dreams, Jeanie heard voices downstairs. It was Sunday morning . . . the day Kenny would leave for Chicago.

Hurriedly she dressed and went down. Kenny was hunched over the kitchen table, still wearing his gold sweater. All his other clothes had been shipped.

"Oh, my goodness! Look at your head!" Kenny's mother exclaimed. The top of Jeanie's head was swollen like a chicken comb. "What will your grandmother say?"

Kenny looked dazed.

Jeanie refused the invitation to have some juice and went to the living room where she could see the driveway and wait for Roy and Gram.

"Here they are!" Jeanie called when she saw Roy's car. She met them at the door and fell, sobbing, into Gram's arms.

Gram embraced her for a moment and then stiffened. "There now!" she said brusquely. "You're bound to be shook up, but you'll be all right!"

Roy offered to take Kenny to the train station. In the car, holding Jeanie's hand tightly, Kenny sat in stunned silence. She had never seem him anything but cheerful and smiling, except for the time he had pneumonia.

And now he had to ride on the train over eight hours—
alone.

At the station Roy and Gram stayed in the car while
Jeanie went in with Kenny. They huddled in a corner,
hands clasped, until they heard the train whistle.

"Don't cry!" Kenny said in a choked voice. He kissed
her quickly. "I'll write."

She got back in the car as the train pulled away and
cried softly most of the way home. She felt as though
she had been dropped into a deep, black well.

Back home, Emma fixed the fire. "Now, you eat a
little something and then you better go to bed. School
tomorrow, you know."

Jeanie groaned. "Oh, Ma! Can't I stay home?"

Gram shook her head. "Don't see why. You're going
to be stiff and sore, but you might as well be stiff and
sore at school rather than mope around home all day."

Fighting tears, Jeanie washed her face while Gram
heated soup. She ate a small bowlful and hobbled up
to her room thinking, *She could be just a little sympathetic!*

Heart thumping, Emma crawled into bed. She
couldn't stop trembling. Poor little girl! Poor little girl!
She wished she could hold her like a two-year-old. But
Jeanie was not two anymore, she was seventeen. Soon
she'd be facing troubles she didn't even know existed.

*I must not baby her! I have to teach her to be strong! Oh,
Lord, it's going to be so hard for her to face everyone
tomorrow. Help her! Help her body to heal, but most of all,
heal her heart. How she's going to miss that boy!*

The Monday morning after the accident, Emma
watched Jeanie make her way across the front lawn
like an arthritic old lady to wait for the school bus.

Oh, dear! I should have let her stay home, Emma
thought. *But life is hard. There will be many, many days in*

her life when she'll have to get up whether she feels like it or not. I don't dare pamper her now.

Jeanie had come downstairs that morning with swollen eyes, but the swelling at the top of her head was gone. When she combed her hair, an alarming amount of hair came out in the comb.

"I'm gonna lose my hair!" she wailed.

"No, it's just hair that was pulled. I'm sure you won't lose much more," Emma reassured her. "How does your head feel this morning?"

"Sore!" Jeanie shouted in Gram's ear, and sat down sullenly to her breakfast of oatmeal. The cereal was covered with the heavy cream Jeanie liked instead of the usual whole milk—Emma's small concession to ease the pain of the morning.

The bus came, and Emma turned to her day's work singing, "Ask the Saviour to help you, comfort, strengthen, and keep you. He is willing to aid you. He will carry you through."

Oh, Lord, she prayed, *carry Jeanie through this day*.

As soon as Jeanie put her books away, she went to find Curly and Pete. They watched her hobble down the corridor toward them.

"Looks like you feel like I do," Pete called to her. "Man! I didn't know I could hurt so many places."

Jeanie stared at Curly's bandage. "Does it hurt a lot?"

"Not anymore. I sure had a headache yesterday, though. How about you?"

Jeanie started to cry.

Pete put an arm around her shoulder and turned her away from the kids passing by. A boy from their class taunted, "That's the way to do it! He smashes up his old man's car and then skips town!"

Jeanie blinked back her tears. "But he was planning to go! His mother had already shipped his clothes!"

"We know that, but a lot of kids don't." Pete gave Jeanie's shoulder a gentle squeeze. "Don't let 'em get you down!"

At lunch time Jeanie told the whole story to Pearl and cried some more. "It's still the shock," Pearl said and squeezed her hand. "You'll feel better tomorrow."

When Jeanie got home, for once Gram didn't say, "Go put an apron on." Instead she asked, "Got a lot of homework?"

Jeanie shook her head.

"That's good. You can get to bed early."

"Oh, sure!" Jeanie mumbled sarcastically. "Now she's concerned about my getting to bed. It didn't bother her to see me drag myself out this morning."

Gram talked good-naturedly while they ate, but Jeanie just picked at her food, excused herself, and sagged into the rocker. She wanted to go up to her room, but she dreaded climbing the stairs.

When Gram finished eating, Jeanie began to set dishes together.

"Oh, just leave those! I'll do them tonight. You do whatever you have to do and get to bed."

Jeanie washed her face thinking, *Beats me! She makes me go to school when I can hardly wiggle, and now she's all sympathetic*. Snuggled in bed, Jeanie wished she could sleep all winter like a bear and wake up graduation morning. There was nothing to look forward to . . . except a letter from Kenny.

But Tuesday and Wednesday passed with no letter. Jeanie choked back her disappointment. No letter Thursday. Jeanie ran upstairs to hide her tears. Friday— a letter! Jeanie tore it open on the spot and read:

> *My dearest Jeanie,*
>
>   *I hope by now you're feeling okay. Boy, was I stiff and sore. I had to go to work Monday morning and I could hardly move.*

I'm working in the shipping department of Garcy Lighting Company. It's okay. It's a job.

Ray and I are going to get a room at the Wilson Ave. YMCA as soon as we save a little money.

Gee, I miss you. I can't wait till Christmas. Tell Pete and Curly hi for me and tell me how Curly looks when she gets her stitches out.

Write soon!

> *Love and lots of kisses,*
> *Your Kenny*

Jeanie wanted to run upstairs and read it over and over, but Gram was standing there waiting expectantly.

"He says his job is okay," she shouted in Gram's ear. "He was stiff and sore, too, and he had to go to work!"

Gram nodded. "That's why I couldn't let you stay home. There are going to be so many times—"

But Jeanie wasn't listening. She was rereading the letter. Her longing for Kenny was unbearable. She went upstairs to her room and closed her eyes to remember the way he looked at her just before he kissed her. She tried to relive those ecstatic moments, but they were always just out of reach.

Finally she began to write. *Dear Kenny* . . . Her pen was almost dry. Sighing, she snapped out the little gold lever on the side of the pen, plunged the tip into the ink bottle, and slowly let the lever go back as the pen filled. If only she could put her feelings into words. Carefully, she rolled the pen on the blotter to absorb the excess ink, made a few circles on a piece of scratch paper, and screwed the top back on the ink bottle.

She stared at the bare branches of the box elder tree by the window, then wrote,

I wonder if you hurt as much as I do. I feel like part of me has been torn away. I go to school and talk to people, but I feel dead inside. I want to be in your arms so badly I don't know what to do!

She had to stop and dry her tears.

I don't know how I'm going to live through this winter. I love you so much. I just want to be with you!

She stared at the window a few moments thinking that she had never hurt so badly in her life. Then she reread what she had written. *Oh, dear! I can't send that!*

She tore it into tiny pieces and threw them into her waste basket. Taking a deep breath and a clean sheet of paper, she started again.

Dear Kenny,

I was glad to get your letter, but you don't sound very excited about your job. How is it going?

Are you getting to see a lot of new things? I bet you wish you had a car. Do you ride the 'El'? Eric told me all about it, and a lot of other things about Chicago. It must be wonderful.

Eric! She realized she had hardly given him a thought since the accident. He would be going back to Chicago soon. He was a nice guy, a lot of fun—but suddenly she knew where her heart was.

It was getting dark. She had better finish her letter. She wrote about Curly and Pete and then ended with "I miss you a lot, but I'm getting used to not seeing you in school. I hope you write often. Love, Jeanie."

Friday evening, Eric came in his dad's car. Jeanie's face felt stiff as she tried to give him a friendly smile.

"I'm going back to Chicago tomorrow," he said. "Care to go for a little ride?"

Jeanie nodded. "Wait till I get a sweater."

"We won't be gone long," she shouted in Gram's ear. "We're just going for a ride."

Jeanie was able to tell Eric all about the accident without crying.

"From what I hear, you kids could have been killed. Is it true that the car hit a boulder when it rolled, and it crushed in the top?"

Now tears threatened. "You wouldn't believe how that car looked. I'm still kinda in shock, I guess. Kenny feels so bad about Curly being cut, I can't imagine how he'd feel if someone had been badly hurt—or killed."

On a high hill Eric pulled over, and they watched the sunset paint a crimson background for the still-colorful autumn leaves. "This has been a special summer," he said, smiling over at her and reaching for her hand. "I wish I didn't have to go back to the city."

"You really like the country, don't you?"

"Let's say I like who lives in the country."

"Eric . . . "

"Look! Don't move!"

A deer was standing not twenty feet from the car.

"It's beautiful," Jeanie whispered.

Eric slipped his arm around her shoulders and slowly drew her close to him.

When they heard a car coming he moved back and started the car, and the deer leaped into the woods.

"We better get back," Jeanie said. It would be easier to tell him at home on the porch swing.

At home, swinging gently, they sat quietly for a few moments—the only sounds the familiar squeak of the swing and chirping of the crickets.

"I hope to come up a few times this winter," Eric said. "And we can write."

"Eric . . . you're such a nice guy, and I like you a lot, but—"

"Uh oh. Here it comes!" he teased. "But what?"

"Eric, be serious. I . . . I can't keep seeing you. It isn't fair to you."

"You mean because of Kenny? I know I'm not the only one in your life. That's all right."

She pulled her hand away. "But it's not all right . . . because I know now where my heart is."

"You're too young, Jeanie! You need to give yourself time!"

"I'm sorry, Eric."

He stood up and gently grasped her arms. "Can I kiss you goodbye?"

She lifted her face.

That night she thought the tears would never stop. Once again she wondered why life had to be so complicated. Part of her wanted to encourage Eric—to be part of his dreams to travel, to fly a plane . . . but her heart was bound inextricably to a cute little guy who would probably never be as tall as she was.

Nine

Autumn's gorgeous colors died like watered flames, leaving a bleak world of ash-gray trees and dry brown grass.

Jeanie didn't even bother to look out of the bus windows these days, unless she stared unseeingly. Like a dull headache that never quite goes away, the ache in her heart never ceased.

Methodically she did her school work. Her classmates, aware of her apathy, sympathized and tried to tease her out of her blues.

Only Gram seemed oblivious to Jeanie's pain. She chattered enthusiastically about Carl's progress on his house, how big the cabbage heads were this year, and countless other irrelevant things. Jeanie sat in glum silence.

Kenny's idea that she come to Chicago and get a job grew stronger in her mind each day. It scared her, of course. She couldn't imagine living in the city. What kind of work could she do?

Occasionally she wandered over to Kenny's house after school and always found a warm welcome. It comforted her to be in his home, close to things that had been familiar to him. On a Friday in October, she walked over to see his mom and was greeted with, "Oh, I'm glad you came! I was going to drive out to see you and your Grandma tomorrow."

Jeanie had never seen those brown eyes so full of excitement.

"How about a fresh cinnamon roll and some milk?" Kenny's mother poured coffee for herself and milk for Jeanie. Then she leaned toward Jeanie. "I'm going to Chicago next week. My nephew Hugo will drive our car. Vi is having another baby, you know, and I plan to bring the older two back home with me until after the baby is born. How would you like to come along?"

For a moment Jeanie was speechless. Then, "Would I ever!" she cried.

"Think your grandma will let you go?"

Jeanie groaned. "Oh, I don't know. . . . How long would we be gone?"

"We plan to leave Friday and come back Tuesday."

"I'd have to miss three days of school."

"How about if I drive out tomorrow afternoon and talk to your grandmother?"

"Would you?" Impulsively, Jeanie jumped up and hugged Kenny's mother, and received a firm hug back.

"I'm not that old! I remember what it was like to be young and in love!"

That evening the bus ride seemed endless. When she finally got home, Jeanie slammed her books down on the table so hard Gram started. Then she pulled her rocker closed to Gram's.

"I went to see Kenny's mother today." Her heart was thumping so hard she could feel it in her ears. "She asked me to go to Chicago with her next weekend!"

"Go to Chicago!" Gram said loudly.

Jeanie put her finger to her lips, then told her as briefly as possible what was planned. She grasped Gram's shoulders. "Can I go? Please, can I go?"

Gram frowned. "Never heard of anything more ridiculous! I can't let you go chasing off and miss school!"

Undaunted, Jeanie continued. "Kenny's mother is coming out to talk to you tomorrow afternoon."

"Hmmph! That won't do any good! You just settle down now." She got up to put wood in the stove. "Never heard of such foolishness!" she muttered, clattering the poker and the stove lid.

Jeanie flew upstairs. "God," she prayed, "I know I don't pray half enough, and I wouldn't blame You if You were put out with me, but I've never wanted anything so bad in my whole life! If You think it's all right for me to go, will You get Gram to change her mind?"

Saturday morning, with Kenny's immaculate home in mind, Jeanie cleaned every surface in view. Gram watched her dip a wet rag in ashes and polish the nickel trim on the stove.

"Nothing like having company to set a person housecleaning," she said with a chuckle. She peeked under the dishtowel that covered the rising *Kuchen* and then glanced at the clock. "When she comes, you go ahead and set the table and make coffee while we talk. I can't be trying to do that and hear at the same time."

When Jeanie heard the car, she was up like a shot and met Kenny's mother at the end of the porch. "It looks like you're going to have to do some talking to convince her." Quietly Jeanie set the table while the two women talked.

"We'll be staying with my daughter," said Kenny's mom. "Ray and Kenny have a place to board now, so there's room." Hastily she added, "And I'll be there all the time! It would be good for Jeanie to see the city and learn about it."

The fragrance of freshly-made coffee filled the room as Jeanie poured it and beckoned for the ladies to come to the table.

Gram passed the plate of *Kuchen* to her guest and said, "I just don't know. What will her teachers say?"

"You know what a good student Jeanie is. Surely she'll be able to make up what she misses."

Gram sighed and took a loud sip of hot coffee.

Eventually the conversation turned to other things, including the threat of war. "Those poor boys," Gram said. "It was bad enough when they were drafted for a year, but now I read it's thirty months! Why, that's almost three years!"

A cold chill raced up Jeanie's spine.

"Tell you what," Gram said when Kenny's mother was ready to leave, "I'll make up my mind by Monday, and Jeanie can run over after school and tell you."

That evening Emma braided her hair at bedtime, her thoughts still fixed on Chicago. *I never thought I'd have to make a decision like this. What on earth will people think if I let her go running off like that? But shame on me! What people think should be the last thing I worry about. It's what is right for Jeanie that matters.*

Sitting on the edge of her bed, she whispered, "Father, You just have to let me know what I should do. How am I supposed to know what's right? I see that sad little face and I want to say, 'Yes! You can go! Be happy!' But I can't let my feelings do the deciding." She rocked back and forth, arms hugging her body, weary but not sleepy.

I wish I could turn off my thoughts like turning off a light. I go round and round and always come back still not knowing what to do.

She got up and paced from window to window, peering out into the long shadows cast by the moonlight where the frozen grass lay waiting for a merciful covering of snow. It would be a long, bleak winter. This trip would be a bright spot for Jeanie.

Back in bed, feeling a bit sleepy now, Emma whispered, "Please help me sleep now and trust that You will let me know what is right when the time comes."

Sunday afternoon Emma lay down for her nap, deeply disappointed. She had expected that somehow the Lord would answer her when she was in prayer in her silent world as the Sunday church service went on around her.

"There are only a few hours left," she reminded Him.

She'd been aware of Jeanie's eyes following her every move all day. "Girl! Stop staring at me!" she had said at dinner. "I feel like a chicken being watched by a hawk! I haven't made up my mind yet!"

Jeanie stomped upstairs and flopped on her bed. *She's just being hateful! She must enjoy seeing me wait and wait! I can't stand this suspense! Why doesn't she say something?*

Back downstairs for supper, Jeanie pleaded, "Will you tell me before I go to bed?"

"I don't know," Gram sighed. "I just don't know."

But when Jeanie had washed her face and was ready for bed, Gram shook her head. "I don't know yet, but I'll know by morning, *Liebchen*." She patted Jeanie's thin little back.

Tears brimmed as Jeanie crept into bed. Gram did care. She had said *Liebchen*. She was just having a hard time deciding. It was easier to go to sleep knowing Gram wasn't just being spiteful.

That night Emma turned and turned in her saggy bed. If only she could talk it over with Ella. She turned over again. *No! It's my responsibility and it has to be my decision. I wonder what Papa would say.*

Whether she was awake or dreaming, she didn't know, but she could see Al so plainly, his bare wrists sticking out past the end of his coat sleeves, rubbing his hands together over the hot stove. She heard him say, "I always remember what that teacher, Tom Blandon, used to say—that a day in town made up for a week of what he could teach a young one in the classroom."

Emma swung her feet out of bed and sat up. "Father? Is that my answer? If it is, I'll trust You to give me Your peace about it."

In the morning Emma didn't even remember lying back down. She had slept peacefully the rest of the night.

Knees feeling weak, Jeanie hurried downstairs. Gram was stirring oatmeal—and smiling! "Think there'll be room in the car for my old straw suitcase?"

"Oh, Mama! I can go?"

Eyes misty, Emma nodded.

"Oh, Mama!" Jeanie sobbed against Gram's neck. "I'll be quiet and helpful. . . ."

"Yes! I want to talk to you about that," Gram said when Jeanie let go. "You know that young woman is about to have a baby. You can't have the least idea how hard it gets toward the last. Don't you make one bit of extra work!"

If only Grace and Ruby were still home! I want to tell somebody! Pearl! Jeanie couldn't wait to get to school.

Giggling and squealing, arms clasped around each other's necks, Jeanie and Pearl danced down the corridor.

"Will Kenny know before you get there?"

"Let's see. . . if I mail a letter tomorrow, he might."

"Maybe you should surprise him."

Jeanie hugged Pearl till she gasped. "Oh, yes! I can't wait to see his face when he sees me!"

The trip seemed to last forever. *I had no idea Chicago was this far away,* Jeanie thought when Kenny's cousin

Hugo said they were almost to Portage, and that was about halfway. He and Kenny's mom talked a lot, but at times Jeanie dozed. She hadn't been able to get to sleep the night before.

Jeanie didn't know what she had expected, but she wasn't prepared for miles and miles of city. Several times they drove through a section of stores and businesses and then houses and then stores again.

"Look over there," Hugo exclaimed. "There's the skyline."

Jeanie caught a glimpse of tall buildings before the buildings close by obscured her view. The buildings became taller and even closer together and not at all attractive. Kenny's mother began to call out street signs.

"That's Sacramento Boulevard, and that's Humboldt Park on the right. Now look for Mozart Street. You'll turn left, Hugo."

When they turned, the street was so narrow with cars parked on both sides that Jeanie was afraid two cars couldn't pass. The tall houses were so close there was only a sidewalk between them, and the front yards were about the size of a porch.

They stopped in front of a high, narrow gray frame house. "Here we are," Kenny's mother said excitedly, and Jeanie tried to smile. In a little while she'd be with Kenny.

They didn't go in the front door but down the sidewalk between the houses to a side door. And there was pretty little Vi, her face round and her eyes a bit puffy, saying, "Hi! Come in!"

Art boomed a greeting, and Merle Ann peeped out from behind him. Little Buddy banged a spoon on the tray of his high chair.

Jeanie greeted them shyly and looked around. She had never seen such high old windows. In the living room there were carved decorations at the top corners of the window above the maroon drapes with big gray plumes. The room was awfully small. However, like Kenny's home, this one was as neat and clean as could be. Not one spot marred the white kitchen table, chairs, stove, and refrigerator.

"I told the boys to come for supper," Vi said, glancing at the clock. "They should be here in half an hour."

Jeanie's heart picked up its tempo. "Kenny doesn't know I'm here, does he?" she asked Vi.

"I don't think so, if you wrote the same time Mother did. I just got her letter today, so he won't have your letter until he gets home tonight."

Jeanie giggled. "I didn't write that I was coming!"

She was glad everyone was talking and playing with the little ones and not paying attention to her. In half an hour Kenny would be here, and she'd feel secure.

When Kenny and Ray arrived, Jeanie stayed in the living room until everyone had greeted each other. Then she slipped into the kitchen and stood behind Art. She caught Kenny's mother's eye and winked.

When Art moved, there she stood—not three feet from Kenny. For an instant he stood motionless, blinking as though he didn't believe what he was seeing.

"Well, I'll be. . . ." Then, with a toss of his head, as if to say, "Folks, this is none of your business," he swung her around the corner back into the living room out of sight as everyone laughed.

After a few hungry kisses he said breathlessly, "Why didn't you tell me you were coming?"

"I wanted to surprise you!" Jeanie giggled. "You should have seen the look on your face!"

He held her so closely she couldn't breathe and whispered, "Oh, Jeanie, I've missed you so much!"

They sat down on the sofa, hands clasped, and Kenny told her about his job and things he had seen in the city. "Are we going to have a time while you're here!"

"Hey, you two!" came Art's gruff voice. "Come and eat! You can't live on love." He patted his firm midriff and laughed. "We tried it, didn't we, Elv? It won't work."

After a great deal of discussion, the guys decided not to go any place special that night but just to drive downtown and look at the skyline.

In the car Kenny said, "Tomorrow I'll take you downtown on the El. I bet my mother will want to come, too. Wait till you see Marshall Fields!"

"What's that?"

"A department store. It's like a whole city by itself."

Jeanie was all but hanging out of the car window looking at the skyscrapers. "Is this the Loop?"

"Yep! See the El tracks?"

"The Chicago Theater," Jeanie read. "Look at all the lights!

"And there's the Tribune Tower all lighted up, and that light going around is the beacon from the Palmolive Building."

Eric had told her about that! Jeanie felt an unexpected pang of sadness. He was the one who had told her about these places . . . she should be seeing them with him. How far away did he live, she wondered. But there was no use thinking about it. His was a different world—one she had chosen not to be part of.

"Hey! Where are you?" Kenny said, pulling her close. "Tired?"

"Uh huh." She leaned her head on his shoulder and closed her eyes. "I see lights and lights and more lights," she murmured. "I didn't think there could be this many lights in the whole world."

"Take a look," Kenny said. "We're on Lake Shore Drive. You can't see much of the lake tonight, but look at the skyline!"

"It's like a picture postcard!"

Jeanie had never seen a church as large as the one they attended the next morning. The hymn book was the same as hers at home, and she could easily follow the order of service, but try as she did to pay attention to the sermon, the pastor's words skimmed over her head, and she struggled to keep awake. A few people nodded as they went out, but they all looked like they were afraid the roast was burning as they rushed off.

After lunch Kenny's mother put her hand on Jeanie's forehead. "You look flushed, but you don't have a fever. Are you all right?"

She nodded uncertainly. "I always get this way when I'm overtired." Her cheeks burned, and her mouth felt dry.

"I think you'd better take a nap and let the boys go to the stadium alone," Kenny's mother said.

"I guess I better do that," Jeanie said wearily. "I wasn't too excited about the rodeo anyway."

"You're sure you don't mind if I go?" Kenny asked.

Jeanie patted his cheek. "I really don't mind. I'm going to sleep."

But she didn't sleep immediately. There was too much to think about since the ride downtown on the El. Those poor people! How could they live in those crowded dirty places? The stores—especially Field's with all its gold, or brass, or whatever it was, and its miles of counters—were wonderful. And the lake! It had been a bit hazy, but she could imagine what it must be like in summer with green grass and blue sky in Grant Park.

A siren startled her. Eerie sound! She heard a street car come to a halt a few blocks away and then start up again. Art was a street car conductor. He had gone off to work that morning, even though it was Sunday, dressed in his navy blue uniform with shoes so shiny you could almost see your face in them.

She sighed and tried to relax. Her heart had quieted down a bit. She was drifting . . . drifting.

Jeanie got up before the boys came home, and Vi suggested that she take a leisurely bath. What luxury to stretch out in a nice, white porcelain tub instead of sitting scrunched up in a round galvanized metal one.

Tuesday morning came too quickly. Every time Jeanie thought of the seven long weeks until Christmas, tears came again. But the trip home went a little faster, thanks to little Buddy and Merle Ann. It was fun to make them laugh.

When she got home that evening, she was so tired it was an effort to shout. Gram asked if she had learned a lot of new things, and Jeanie tried describe some of the things she had seen. But Gram seemed more interested in the people than the places.

"Kenny said to thank you for letting me come."

Gram smiled and nodded. "It won't be long now till Christmas."

Jeanie groaned. Not long! It was seven weeks away.

One night in November, Emma watched Jeanie snatch Kenny's letter and, without so much as a nod of greeting, dash upstairs. Poor love-sick little girl!

Jeanie paid little attention to Roy's children these days, although she did love to hold little Arne and sing to him. When Emma did see Jeanie talking with Helen, they always appeared to be arguing. Not being able to hear what they were saying disturbed her.

As Emma scraped carrots to put into the soup, she prayed, "Oh, Father, all she thinks about is that boy! I know You had to make male and female so they would be attracted to each other, but did You have to make the attraction that strong?"

Try as she might to interest Jeanie in the lives of others, her words rarely evoked a comment, question, or even a smile. "Might as well talk to the wall," Emma muttered.

At least she had been keeping up with her school work. Her report card had been good—Emma had been tempted to compliment her on it, but quickly checked herself. *Don't want the girl to be overconfident.*

But Emma's main concern was that there was little room for God in Jeanie's life.

The Sunday before Thanksgiving, Pastor Zaremba came over after church and asked Jeanie to take charge of the Christmas program. Emma was delighted. Now Jeanie would have to give God some thought.

She knitted contentedly that weekend, glancing up now and then to watch Jeanie working at the table with the pile of material the pastor had left for her. There was life in her eyes again.

Jeanie came over and sat down next to Emma, her eyes sparkling with enthusiasm. "Oh, Mama! It's going to be the best program ever! I'm going to have the little ones do lots of singing and speaking. I'm not going to give long recitations to the big kids. They hate getting up there to speak—but they'll sing together."

Emma smiled encouragingly. "That sounds nice. I always like to see the little ones."

"Do you think little Arne could sing? He's only two."

"Why don't you ask Helen?"

Sewing a dress for Christmas also helped Jeanie pass the time. She ordered some bright red rayon flannel and got to work. The pattern she chose was more complicated than she had anticipated, however, and over and over she had to rip out her work and start over. She ruined the collar so badly she had to cut a new one. One night she threw it aside, completely exasperated.

"You're just tired tonight. It will go better when you try again," Gram assured her.

The next evening Jeanie dreaded even to think of all the ripping she had to do. Why had she ever chosen that pattern? But when she picked it up to begin working, she found the pieces ripped apart and neatly folded—ready to be sewn again.

"Oh, Mama! Thank you," she shouted, squatting down beside Gram. "You don't know how I dreaded ripping all that again!"

Gram smiled, nodded, and winked—an endearing combination that always flooded Jeanie with affection for her. Carefully she lined up the seams and lowered the presser foot. Gram could be so dear—so thoughtful and kind. It made Jeanie feel horribly guilty for all the times she felt so angry at her scolding and frowning.

When the seam came out right, Jeanie showed Gram, who nodded and smiled as if to say, "I knew you could do it!"

When Jeanie got on the bus Monday morning, December eighth, it seemed like everyone was talking and yelling at the same time. She heard "Pearl Harbor" and "ships bombed" and "those sneaky Japs" and didn't know what was going on. She sat down next to Carol, a classmate from Spirit.

"What's all the excitement?"

"You mean you don't know? The Japanese bombed our fleet at Pearl Harbor. Just about wiped it out! President Roosevelt will address Congress today, and they'll declare war on Japan."

War! For a moment Jeanie couldn't reply. Anger welled up within her, at Japan, at Hitler, at anyone or anything that had caused this turn of events.

That morning the principal brought a radio into the assembly room. They waited in stunned silence for President Roosevelt's message.

All day the conversation centered around the war. Two teachers who were in the reserves announced that they would leave immediately. Spike's two brothers were in Pearl Harbor, and his family was waiting to hear if they were all right.

That night Jeanie told Gram she wanted to order an electric radio, so it would be there when the electricity was turned on. Roy agreed, and Jeanie ordered the radio she had been looking at in the Montgomery Ward catalog for months.

On December eleventh, Germany and Italy declared war on the United States. The village of Rib Lake felt the stark reality when news came that Spike's brother Lee had been killed and Chuck badly wounded. Every family with young men in service lived in dread of the words: "We regret to inform you. . . . "

As days went by, new words and terms like rationing, U-boat, maneuvers, paratroopers, and aircraft carrier were fast becoming part of everyday conversation—as well as 1-A and 4-F. Men received their draft notices and went for their physical examinations. They were classified 1-A if they were fit to serve, and 4-F if they failed to pass. Would Kenny's height keep him out of service? He was only five foot three and a half. Maybe, just maybe, his short stature would turn out to be a blessing.

On December twenty-second, President Roosevelt signed a new Selective Service Act under which all men from eighteen to sixty-four years of age had to register, and all men from twenty to forty-four were subject to conscription.

Jeanie prayed fervently that the war would end before Kenny got drafted. She couldn't stand even to think about his going into service.

Ten

On Christmas Eve, candles flickered in the church windows. The fragrance of the fresh balsam tree greeted the people as they entered. Soon there was hardly a vacant seat.

The excited children scuffled and giggled, and with considerable effort Jeanie settled them in the first three pews.

With a confident smile, Pastor Zaremba turned the service over to Jeanie. Through recitations and songs, the beautiful story of Christ's birth was told again. Facing smiling faces, little Arne obligingly sang his verse of "Away in the Manger," but a little later in the program, when Jeanie called on him to sing his second song, he lounged on the carpeted steps with the other little ones. "Naw," he returned. "I singed one already."

After the service, the children received their bags of candy and nuts, and people milled around and visited. "What a lovely program!" they said. "One of the nicest we ever had!" To Gram they shouted, "You must be very proud of that girl!" and Gram nodded modestly.

Jeanie basked in the praise, but she didn't prolong any conversations, for she was eager to get home. Kenny was coming!

At home she paced nervously. Kenny had gone to church with his parents at Rib Lake, but he should arrive soon. She had trimmed the tree earlier in the afternoon and was eager to light the candles, but she didn't want them to burn down before he came.

Car lights in the driveway! Her heart set up a clamor. Before he had a chance to knock, she raced to the door and opened it. There he stood, with that appealing smile, the tip of his nose red with the cold, wearing a new camel-hair overcoat.

He kissed her quickly, then greeted Gram while Jeanie lit the candles on the tree. Gram admired the glowing tree for a few moments, then turned to Jeanie and Kenny. "You kids enjoy it," she said. "It's my bedtime."

She was hardly out of the room before Kenny gathered Jeanie into his arms. "I thought Christmas would never come!"

"We could sit down, you know!" Jeanie said, dizzy with kisses.

He turned her rocker so that it faced the tree and pulled her down on his lap. "The candles look nice, but aren't you afraid they'll catch fire to the tree?"

Jeanie shook her head. "Never have yet. We don't ever leave the tree when the candles are burning. We have candles on the big trees at church and at school."

"That scares me!"

Jeanie giggled. "I didn't think anything scared you!" She slipped off his lap and handed him his gift.

He looked at it. "A shirt, I bet," he said with a grin.

Jeanie shook her head. "Guess again."

"Why guess when I can open it?" He tore off the paper. "A robe! I can use that. At the Y, we have to go down the hall to the bathroom." He gave her a thank you kiss, then he leaned over and reached into his overcoat pocket for a package about six inches long, which he handed to Jeanie.

Hardly glancing at the wrapping, she tore off the paper and opened the red case. "A watch! Oh, it's beautiful! Rose gold!"

He helped her take it out of the case, clasped the maroon cord band on her wrist, and showed her how to adjust the size. "I set it this afternoon," he said, sounding pleased with himself. "Do you really like it?"

"Oh, I do! I do!"

He laughed. "Are you practicing for our wedding?"

"Sure! Why not!" she said flippantly.

Kenny kissed her again. "I wish I could have given you a ring," he said softly, "but everyone would have a fit if you got one before you graduate." He laughed. "I couldn't afford one, anyway!"

"That's all right. We know what this gift means, and that's all that matters."

"I can't stay long tonight. Ma wants me home, but she wants to know if you can come tomorrow afternoon. We're having relatives over, and you could stay for the evening. Will that be all right with your grandma?"

"I think so. We're going to Carl and Olga's for dinner. They're in their new house now, you know. You could pick me up there."

He got up and put on his overcoat and held her close again. "Oh, Jeanie. We're going to have years and years of Christmases together!" he said huskily. "Go to bed now and dream about *our* Christmas tree."

When Jeanie met Kenny's grandmother the next day, she understood why Kenny and his father were so short. The little lady was barely four feet tall and just about as wide! She wore her white hair twisted in a bun on top of her head. Her hearing was fine, but her eyes had a milky look to them, and Kenny said she couldn't see very well.

They walked into the living room to see the tree. "It's beautiful," Jeanie exclaimed. "I've never seen a blue and silver Christmas tree before!" The blue lights glowed serenely, and the silver and blue balls reflected the lights of the candles on the table.

Kenny's mother beamed Jeanie a smile.

It was a laughter-filled day, but Jeanie would have preferred to spend more time alone with Kenny. She knew he felt the same.

"Two more days!" he said when he took Jeanie home. He had to catch the train again Sunday morning.

Two days! Jeanie thought again when she snuggled into bed that night . . . and then almost five months until graduation. How could she endure it?

They made good use of their two days, tobogganing with their school friends and visiting with Grace and Ruby. On Saturday they laughed and dreamed by the wood stove, talking about *their* home and *their* kids.

"I may be gone a while, you know," Kenny said. "Sometimes I think I should enlist and get it behind me."

Jeanie clung to him as if holding him back. "Don't even think about enlisting! Maybe the war will be over, and you'll never have to go!"

It was torture saying goodbye, knowing they wouldn't see each other for five long months. "Maybe you could come home for Easter," Jeanie suggested.

"If we want to get married, I have to save some money," Kenny said. "I'd have to take at least one day off from work, and I'd have to work a whole week for the train fare."

Jeanie pouted. "Why weren't we born rich?" Sobbing quietly, she watched the car drive out of the driveway, past the house, and up the hill until it was out of sight. As she was about to turn off the light, she saw Kenny's white scarf lying on a chair. Holding it close, she carried it upstairs, breathing in the fragrance of his after-shave lotion.

In the morning she was still holding it.

January first. Emma took down the old calendar, rolled it up and put it in the stove, and hung a new one in its place. Less than five months till Jeanie would graduate. *And that girl is supposed to go out in the world and work?* Emma thought. *She can't even remember to take her clothes upstairs.*

She sighed and sat down with her knitting. Time and again through the past weeks, when she had told Jeanie to do something—like bring in a pail of water or empty the slop pail—it was like Jeanie was the deaf one.

"I'll wash the dishes," Emma would say, "and you bring in a pail of water."

Jeanie would nod in agreement, then sit down and start to read. Emma would do the dishes, and still Jeanie hadn't moved.

"Don't forget to get that water," Emma would say, not wanting to scold.

A half hour would pass. An hour. And there Jeanie sat, nose in her book, rocking away. "You go get that water now!" Emma would say a bit more sternly.

Emma would take her hair down and braid it. Still no water. "Go and get that water now!" she would shout. "I ask you to do one simple little thing, and you put it off and put it off! How are you ever going to hold a job if you can't do what little I ask you to do here?"

"Oh, for crying out loud! I'll get the water!" Jeanie would slam her book down and flounce out the door, clanging the pail against the door frame.

Emma thought about a dozen similar scenes. What was she doing wrong? And what was the solution?

"I feel like a total failure," she confided to Ella one day. "I just don't know how that girl will manage out in the world. Land knows, I've tried to teach her to be responsible!"

"Oh, Ma! She'll do fine. Remember how well she took care of things here when I was gone last summer?"

"Hmmph. Well, I don't know. Maybe she'll have more ambition when she's on her own. None of you children were that way—except Hank."

Ella chuckled. "Ma! We weren't a bit different! You've just forgotten. And there were so many of us that you were too busy to see it all!"

Emma sighed a sigh of resignation. "That's what Clara told me once, but it seems like I need to hear it again. I sure hope you're right!"

Each evening when the bus started down the long hill, and the house and barn came into view, Jeanie's stomach would tighten. She dreaded opening the door. She couldn't even get her coat off before Gram would say, "Now, go put an apron on!"

From then on it was: "Don't leave that stuff lay there! Take it upstairs. . . . Look at that puddle! You didn't sweep off your overshoes before you came in. . . . Get started with your homework, so you aren't sitting up all hours. . . . Pick up your threads when you get done sewing!"

Bouncing down the hill on the rutted road, Jeanie grumbled to herself. "She doesn't care about me. Does she ever ask how things are going for me? No! All she cares about is getting things done—right now!"

Jeanie picked up her trombone and school bag as the bus slowed to a stop. It would be a long time till spring.

Day after January day remained locked in winter's firm grip. Frost from Jeanie's breath edged her comforter each morning, and the water in the glass on the nightstand was often frozen solid . . . even though Gram put wood in the stove almost hourly through the night.

Each evening Jeanie laid out her clothes so she could grab them, run down, bathe quickly, and dress by the open oven door. Even though Kenny wasn't there to look good for, she never wore the same outfit two days in a row, and her hair was always clean and set each evening in aluminum rollers.

Gram would watch her roll up her hair. "How on earth can you sleep in those things?" she would say, shaking her head.

Jeanie would shrug and continue rolling. Because she wore her hair swept up at the sides and pinned in a roll with bobby pins, it wasn't necessary to have rollers on the sides. Rollers in the back and on top were no problem!

One morning in the middle of January, Jeanie winced as a pain shot around her ribs and over her left shoulder as she was getting dressed. Not pleurisy again, she thought. Back in grade school, she had suffered with it for weeks at a time.

"Must be an inherited weakness," Gram had said. She often had bouts of it, too.

Jeanie finished dressing with only a few twinges of pain, hoping it would go away completely. When she saw the bus coming, she wrapped her scarf over her mouth and hurried out. The wind howled around the corner of the house, and the subzero temperature made the snow squeak underfoot. The icy air made her gasp, even with a scarf over her face.

She slid her trombone case under an empty seat and flopped down as the bus lurched forward. In the usual din of shouting and laughter, no one heard her cry out in pain. Huddled in the hard seat, she tried to take shallow breaths, knowing that the deeper she breathed the more pain she would have.

Why didn't I stay home? she thought, choking back tears, but she knew the answer all too well. When the weather was warm enough for her to be up in her room, staying home was fine. But now, when her room was so cold she could do nothing but burrow deep under the covers, staying home meant sitting next to Gram in the rocker or lying in Gram's bed, listening . . . listening to Gram's loud throat-clearing and talking to Helen and, worst of all, her constant humming and singing. Going to school in pain was definitely preferable.

But at band practice, when Jeanie tried to lift her arms to play, the pain was so severe she almost dropped her horn. Mr. Spiedel scowled at her, but then saw that she was in distress and didn't scold. "Come to practice," he told her later, "and play whenever you can."

By evening there was no hiding the pain from Gram.

"Not pleurisy again! You'll have to stay home until it gets better."

Jeanie didn't argue. She ate a little supper and crept into Gram's bed until Gram's bedtime. Then, wearing her heavy old blanket-cloth bathrobe over her pajamas, she dragged herself upstairs and shivered her way under the covers.

Jeanie spent most of the next day in Gram's bed, thankful to lie still, keeping one ear tight against the pillow and holding the other shut with her finger. She wanted to pray, but the guilt from feeling so ugly toward Gram hung too heavy. She felt like a dog cowering with its tail between its legs.

At times she dozed, but then her arm would fall and she'd hear the quavery humming and have to hold her ear shut again.

Her morning work finished, Emma poked her head around the corner of the door to see how Jeanie was. Her face was turned toward the wall, the comforter pulled over the back of her head. Emma sighed. No sense disturbing her.

She picked up her knitting and sat down heavily in her rocker. She had planned to spin today, but the clunk, clunk, of the spinning wheel would be aggravating for Jeanie. She certainly didn't want to give that poor girl any more misery.

Father, what can I do for her? she prayed silently. *If the doctor could do anything for her, I'd have Roy take us in, but all he ever tells me to do is rest. If only it was like in the Bible, when You touched people and they were healed.* She shook her head. *I don't understand, Lord. You are the same God! Couldn't you do that, even now?*

The fire! How could she have forgotten to put wood in the stove before she sat down? With a grunt, she heaved herself out of the rocker and put three sticks in as quietly as she could.

When Jeanie got up to eat some soup at noon, Emma watched her closely for signs of pain. "Any better?" she asked.

Jeanie nodded, ate her soup quickly, and went back to bed without talking.

Roy stopped by a litle later. "I have to go to Phillips tomorrow," he said. "Do you want to go and visit Nora? I'm dropping Helen and the children at her sister's."

"My goodness, it's been months since I've been to Len and Nora's," Emma replied. "I sure would like to go. But it depends on how Jeanie's feeling. "

Huddled by the oven door, Jeanie tried to convince Gram to go. "I'll be fine!" she shouted, silently praying, *Lord, please have Gram go tomorrow!* She knew it was a selfish prayer—she was much more interested in having a quiet day to herself than in Gram's having a visit with Len and Nora.

Gram changed her mind three times before she finally decided to go. When the car was finally out of sight—with Gram in it—an elated feeling swept over Jeanie. Even though the pain still shot around her ribs and occasionally over her shoulder, she felt like being up and doing something. Reading didn't take arm movement, so she sat on the oven door and finished the last two chapters of *Wuthering Heights*.

It was wonderful to linger over her sandwich at noon and to lie quietly in bed without having to plug her ears. Now and then the fire snapped and the wind whistled around the corner, and sometimes a window-pane rattled.

Music! That was what she wanted!

With her bathrobe tied tightly around her and woolen socks on her feet, she lifted the lid of the phonograph in Roy and Helen's living room. "Girl of My Dreams"—she'd start with that one.

Slowly she turned the crank to wind the spring, ignoring the twinges of pain, and set the needle on the record. The familiar notes rang out. Smiling, she sat down in the big old black leather rocker and leaned her head back. Thoughts of Kenny flooded her mind as the romantic strains filled the room. *Oh, what I'd give to hear him say "I love you" right now!*

All too soon the song ended, and all she could hear was the scratching of the needle as it went round and round the grooves at the end of the record. She squatted down and hunted through the records stored below the phonograph. Band marches by John Phillip Sousa. That would be fun. The lively music filled the room.

Maybe there'll be a letter from Kenny today, she thought. But she wouldn't dare go out to the mailbox in this icy wind. Gram would have a fit!

But if she took only the letter from Kenny and left the rest of the mail, no one would know she had gone out.

She hardly heard the band marches, she was so busy arguing with herself.

I'll dress real warm!

But what if someone sees your tracks?

I want that letter!

Gram says that learning to wait for things is part of growing up.

Jeanie wound the spring again, selected Irving Berlin's "Always," and put the needle on. Of all the goals she had set, acting like a grownup was at the top. She nodded her head resolutely. She'd wait.

She let the lovely notes flow over her and the beautiful words penetrate her mind. *That's how it will be with Kenny and me . . . when the things I've planned need a helping hand he will understand . . . always . . . and I'll do the same for him.*

If only records ran longer than a couple minutes! It seemed like a song just started and she had to jump up and turn the record over.

She dreamed her way through "Together" and "My Blue Heaven," Kenny's face before her. How many times had she traced the curve of his lip with her finger, smoothed those heavy eyebrows, run her finger down that straight nose? Loneliness overwhelmed her. How would she survive all the weeks ahead?

Suddenly she felt too exhausted to wind the machine one more time. She put the records away, crawled back into bed, and sobbed.

On Monday she felt well enough to go back to school. Once her make-up work was handed in, Jeanie was able to get back to doing what she really enjoyed— reading *Good Housekeeping* magazine during study hall. She pored over every article about being a good homemaker and wife. She even read the ones about babies, although she didn't expect to need that information for a long while.

The new automatic washers and dryers fascinated her. Imagine just putting clothes in a machine to get them washed, and not even having to put them through a wringer! And what would it be like to stuff wet things into another machine and have them come out dry? The article said they came out softer than when line-dried in the wind.

When they were assigned to write a short story for English class, Jeanie spent hours thinking about it. She wrote a story about a young married couple having a misunderstanding and how it turned out all right. She hoped for an A and was elated when the paper came back with an A+. She let Pearl read it and, when Pearl told other girls about it, the story was passed on and on. For over a week, girls came up to her and told her she should be a writer.

On the school bus she thought about that . . . but if she were a writer, she'd have to type. Ugh. Anyway, she didn't know the first thing about how a person became a published author. She turned her thoughts back to what she did know about: getting married and having her own home. What could be more important than being a good homemaker, wife, and mother?

But it had felt good to have the girls praise her story. She decided to make the effort to tell Gram about it. While Gram watered her plants on the table in her bedroom, Jeanie hovered close to her left ear and told her how the A+ story had been passed around. "The girls say I should be a writer when I grow up!"

"Hmmph!" Gram said impatiently. "I think you'd do better to spend your time studying world history, instead of writing silly stories!" She reached over and pinched off a tip of the red begonia.

Jeanie stamped her foot in frustration. Jabbing a finger at the plant, she shouted at Gram, "That's exactly what you do to me! You just can't stand to have me feel good about anything I do! Every time I get a compliment, you cut me down—just the way you cut down that plant!"

Gram took a step back from Jeanie's angry face. "What on earth are you talking about?"

Jeanie didn't even care how loud she yelled. "All you ever do is tell me what I do wrong!" Tears ran unheeded, and she sobbed between the words. "I must do *something* right once in a while! But I don't ever remember you praising me! I don't even care what I do anymore! It's never good enough, anyway!"

Gram staggered backward a few steps and sat down hard on the edge of her bed. Then she caught her breath, leaned forward, and pulled Jeanie's sleeve, motioning for her to sit on the chair next to the bed.

Jeanie's eyes blazed, and angry words continued to spew out. "It isn't my fault I was born! I couldn't help it that my mother died because of it! I know I'll never be perfect like she was, but you could at least give me a chance! Other people like me! Why can't you?"

Gram's jaw hung slack. "But I didn't mean . . . I never knew you felt like this. I just don't want you to grow up vain and haughty—and careless." It was her turn for tears. "Oh, girl, if you only knew how much I care about you!"

Jeanie gave a wry laugh that ended with a sob. "Well, you sure have a funny way of showing it!" She jumped up and ran upstairs, ignoring Gram's order to come back.

How those words stung. "You'd do better to spend your time studying world history instead of writing silly stories!" Not one word about the A+! Not one word about how the girls enjoyed her story!

Jeanie cried until she couldn't cry anymore. Her breath still catching in little sobs, she rolled over and gazed at the graceful lines of the white daisies on her coral wallpaper. She loved that wallpaper. How happy she had been when Gram and Helen papered it to go with Jeanie's mother's ivory bedroom set, which had come to her after her dad died.

"I bet I have the prettiest room in the whole county!" she had said to Gram as they hung white ruffled curtains at the window.

Gram had nodded, winked, and smiled all at one time, and Jeanie had known she was happy, too.

Suddenly Jeanie remembered all the times she had seen Gram acknowledge her with that nod, wink, and smile combination when she walked into a room at some family or church gathering. It always made her feel special . . . loved.

Now the angry words she had shouted at Gram haunted her. Deep down she knew Gram cared about her. But why couldn't she show it? Her anger surged all over again.

Emma rocked in agony. *What have I done? She looked at me like she hates me! Oh, Lord! Help me!*

She sobbed into her apron, recalling Jeanie's angry words.

Poor little girl! How could she think I don't care for her? But the way she talked to me! Such disrespect! I never let any of my children talk to me like that! I should call her down, right here and now, and make her apologize.

Emma blew her nose and wearily, shakily got to her feet. She simply didn't have the energy to demand an apology.

She put wood in the stove and pulled the soup kettle over to the front lid. *Better let well enough alone for right now. Maybe I can talk to Ella about it.*

She set the table, and when the soup was hot she called, "Jeanie! Supper's ready!" just as she always did.

Jeanie thumped her heel to let Gram know she had heard, but she didn't hurry down. Huddled at the window, she tried to decide how to act.

On the way downstairs she thought, *I'll just see what she has to say.*

Steam was curling up from the bowl at her place when she sat down. Any minute now Gram would say, "Be careful now! It's hot!"

Gram eased herself into a chair. "Be careful now! It's hot!"

I'm not a baby! I can see that it's hot! Chills raced up Jeanie's spine as Gram noisily slurped her hot soup. She wanted to throw something—to scream—to run! She scraped back her chair and shouted, "I gotta go!"

She didn't go through Helen and Roy's rooms to reach the outhouse, the way she usually did. Surely the whole household had heard what was going on, and another scolding she didn't need.

Sobbing and shivering, she sat in the dark refuge. *I wish I could die! Right now!*

Then she remembered Kenny's smiling face. The way he winked. The way he whispered, "I love you, Jeanie!"

With a shuttering sigh, she latched the door behind her and went back to the house. Just a few more months. Somehow she'd endure it.

The winter wore on. Every evening after supper, Jeanie dried dishes, carried in water and took out the slop pail, and then began her homework. If only it would turn warm, so she could work upstairs.

It wasn't bad while Gram was up knitting. She didn't sing or hum very much at night and, when she did, Jeanie sang loud enough to drown her out. But when Gram went to bed and began praying, Jeanie fled upstairs in the cold or sat with her fingers in her ears. She had no desire to eavesdrop on Gram's prayers. She would wait and wait, fingers in her ears, checking occasionally to see if Gram was done. What on earth did she find to pray about that long?

Spring couldn't come a day too soon.

Emma's thoughts circled round and round. How could Jeanie think she didn't care about her? Couldn't the child see how hard she worked to keep her clothes clean? How, with money so scarce, she saw that Jeanie had things she needed while making do herself with what she had? Couldn't Jeanie understand that the scolding was for her benefit—that she was trying to teach her to be a responsible person?

Emma poured out the dishwater, wiped the dish pan, and hung it up. She hadn't even thought about what she'd do today. Gently, she drew the door to Helen's living room shut and sat down in her rocker—without her knitting. Try as she would to justify the scolding and the canceled-out compliments, she knew they had hurt Jeanie deeply.

In a few weeks, she would be gone. "Oh, Father! What have I done?" Emma whispered. "I never dreamed she felt like I didn't care about her. What could I have done differently? I was just trying to help her be good."

She leaned her head back, took her glasses off, and let the tears run as images of Jeanie's angry face loomed before her. She thought again of talking to Ella, but abandoned that idea with a sigh. Ella would be too tactful to say, "I told you so!" but she wouldn't offer much sympathy, either. Emma remembered what she had said before—Jeanie was no different from Emma's own children, and she paid too much attention to the girl's shortcomings.

"Lord, it's just You and me," Emma concluded. "Somehow You have to show me how to make things right with Jeanie and teach me what I'm supposed to do." She shook her head and got up to put wood in the stove. *Just goes to show that a person can have a whole bunch of children and still not know how to raise them*, she thought.

Jeanie remained aloof. For once she had the upper hand, and she wasn't about to relinquish it. It didn't make her feel good to see Gram looking so wounded, though.

In English class the teacher interrupted her musings. "Who knows the meaning of the word ambivalent?"

Ambivalent! The word sent a little shock through Jeanie. If anyone knew the meaning of that word, she certainly did, but she wasn't about to use her own situation as an example.

"Doesn't anyone know the meaning of the word ambivalent?" the teacher asked again.

When no one responded, Jeanie raised her hand. "It means to feel two different ways about the same thing."

"That's right, Jeanie. Can you give us an example?"

"Well . . . I want to go and work in Chicago after I graduate, but I still want to be home."

The class discussion went on to other subjects, but Jeanie's thoughts stayed on ambivalence. Knowing the meaning of the word didn't help a bit. What she really needed to know was what to do with her ambivalent feelings.

As much as she wanted to go to Chicago, to be with Kenny and start a new life, tears came to her eyes whenever she thought of Gram being alone. Not actually alone in the house, of course—but she wouldn't have anyone depending on her—no one to cook for, to wait for—to scold! All these years Gram had virtually lived for her and now—

But she couldn't stay home! She simply couldn't! Gram wasn't going to change. She'd continue to pick at every little thing and point out Jeanie's faults whenever someone said something nice.

The bell rang, and everyone rushed out of the classroom. Jeanie tagged along behind. *Only two more months. Somehow I'll get through them.*

That evening when Gram tried to start a conversation, Jeanie answered in monosyllables. She did her chores and her homework, and when she finished her skin care routine she gave Gram a dutiful peck on the cheek and went upstairs to write to Kenny. Gram hadn't scolded quite as much, she noticed, and that she appreciated—but when she cuddled into bed and tried to pray, all she could see was Gram's furrowed brow.

As Emma sat on the edge of the bed that night and tried to pray, for once words didn't come. In a way she felt like she should ask God to forgive her, but that didn't make any sense. She had only done what she thought was right for Jeanie.

She shivered and pulled the quilt up around her shoulders. "Father," she prayed. "I sure am mixed up. Seems like my whole world is upside down. I just can't believe that what I've been doing all these years with the best intentions could have been wrong." She let her breath out with a groan. "But if I am wrong, I trust You to show me what to do now."

Eleven

In March a classmate ran up to Jeanie in the hallway. "I hear you plan to go to Chicago after you graduate," she said. "Do you have a job?"

Startled, Jeanie shook her head.

"My sister Pat has been working as a housekeeper, but she's getting married. The lady she works for asked if she could find a replacement. Are you interested?"

Jeanie took the sister's address, and an exchange of letters began. The employer, Mrs. Winston, was a divorced working woman with a lovely home in Skokie, according to Pat.

Jeanie replied that she would be interested and waited for an answer. It came just before her birthday, March 31. Mrs. Winston agreed that Jeanie could take Pat's place.

Kenny's mother had invited Jeanie and Pearl for a birthday lunch, and Jeanie could hardly wait to tell her the news.

"Tell you what," Kenny's mother said, her brown eyes sparkling with excitement across the beautifully set table, "I want to go and visit Vi. Maybe we can ride down on the train together. What day is graduation?"

"May fourteenth!" both girls said simultaneously.

"When do you want to leave?"

The very word set Jeanie's stomach aflutter. "Ah . . . I hadn't thought about it. Maybe the next week."

Jeanie told Gram her plans.

"So soon!" Gram said. "I was hoping you'd stay home for another month at least."

"Pat wants to quit as soon as possible to get ready for her wedding. If I want that job, I'll have to go as soon as I can."

Gram nodded without lifting her head. "I know," she said.

"I'm still not ready for her to go," Emma told the Lord that night. "Especially now, with such a strain between us. I thought by the time she graduated, I'd feel like she was ready to be on her own—but she's the same scatterbrain as she was two years ago. How will she manage to hold a job?" She felt a lump forming in her throat. "Will she leave home still thinking that I scolded just to make life miserable for her?"

It was Saturday, April eighteenth—Gram's seventy-third birthday. Jeanie got up earlier than usual to help Gram clean the house before company came.

They had the chairs all moved to one side of the room and were washing the floor when Carl came to the door.

"Happy birthday!" he shouted and handed Gram half a dozen downy-stemmed mayflowers he had found in the woods.

"Oh, my goodness!" she exclaimed. "We are going to have an early spring." She took the old toothpick holder out of the cupboard.

Carl nodded and grinned. "I better get going. Looks like you two are busy."

"Oh, come sit down! We'll get done in time. I expect the girls will be coming over. Helen is baking a cake."

Jeanie continued to dust chairs, thinking how disturbed Gram would be if she wanted to visit with someone in the midst of their cleaning. She watched Gram's eyes light up as Carl told her about his plans for the spring. She just listened . . . and didn't even reach for her knitting.

Smiling to herself, Jeanie quietly put the chairs back around the table. Someday, if I have sons, I want to take time for them the way Gram does and listen to their plans and be part of their lives.

By two o'clock Ella, Mamie, Sadie, Olga, Helen, Gram, and Jeanie were seated around Helen's huge round table. Jeanie watched Gram smile and nod when someone shouted to her, but she knew Gram heard only part of what was said. Nevertheless, she maintained an eager, interested expression and a serene smile. Later, Jeanie knew, she would stagger with exhaustion and say, "I'm more tired than if I had cleaned a whole house."

Jeanie looked around at these women who were such an important part of her life. Gram, she realized, would not be alone with her lonesome feelings in the days to come. Jeanie sensed a deep sadness in Aunt Mamie, even though she laughed as heartily as ever. Paul and Art had gone into service, and Ruby was in Milwaukee. Aunt Ella, too, talked about how much she missed her girls. Although Sadie still had younger children at home, her older ones were leaving.

Nothing stays the same! Jeanie thought.

Helen brought the cake to the table with seven lighted candles on one side and three on the other.

Tears blurred Jeanie's vision as they sang "Happy Birthday." Would this be the last time she would be part of Gram's birthday celebration?

While she was clearing the table, Olga came over to put a handful of silverware into the dishwater. "You look like you're ready to cry," she observed. "What's the matter?"

Jeanie gulped and caught a tear with the back of her dripping hand. "This could be the last time I'll be at Gram's birthday party."

Olga squeezed her arm. "So . . . maybe you won't be here in person. But don't you know that it's not the miles between two people that matter?"

Jeanie looked down at tiny Olga questioningly.

"If two people don't get along, they can sit right at the same table and not really be close."

Thoughtfully, Jeanie washed a plate. Yes. That was true. Olga had no idea how far apart she and Gram were right now.

Olga grabbed a dishtowel and spoke in low tones that went unheeded by the others in the room. "Don't let emotions rule you these last weeks at home. Life changes. We leave some things and go on to others. We can't have both."

Jeanie pondered that conversation as she took a walk down to the bridge that evening. Again, as so many times in the past, Olga had given her a new perspective. Like lifting a pan from the heat when it was about to boil over, Olga had settled Jeanie's emotions back where they belonged.

We can't have both, she reminded herself.

If it hadn't been for all the sewing Jeanie planned to do before she left, the weeks certainly would have dragged. Gram agreed that they could keep the sewing machine in their room, even though it was a bit crowded, instead of having to move it from Helen's kitchen each time she wanted to sew.

As usual, Jeanie improvised and combined patterns she already owned instead of buying new ones. For several skirts and blouses it had worked well, but for a copen blue two-piece dress with a tailored collar, things weren't working out.

The Saturday after Gram's birthday, Jeanie sewed and ripped, sewed and ripped until, at suppertime, she tossed the pieces in a heap. She wasn't even tempted to work at it the next day. Had it been going well, she might have tried to talk Gram into letting her sew on Sunday.

Not that Gram was legalistic about not working on Sunday—she simply agreed that, whenever possible, everyone needed a day out of the harness. "God knew what He was doing," she'd say. "We're wise to pay attention to what He says for our own good."

So Monday evening on the bus, instead of looking forward to an evening of sewing, Jeanie dreaded tackling that pesky neckline again. She'd probably have to spend most of the evening ripping.

"Now, go put an apron on!" Gram said as soon as Jeanie walked through the door.

"How come I feel sad about leaving?" Jeanie muttered to herself.

Gram drained the boiled potatoes and said, "You get your homework done before you start sewing!"

Jeanie's jaws tightened.

She hated Gram.

She loved Gram!

Gram was her mother, her provider—the one who never even ate an orange without insisting that Jeanie take more than half. She hung wet clothes out in freezing weather, carefully mended and ironed and folded all Jeanie's things, scrambled eggs just the way Jeanie liked them, skimmed off heavy cream for her oatmeal—anything she could think of to get her to eat breakfast.

And Jeanie couldn't stand to sit at the same table with her! Just about everything Gram did irritated her.

How she hated to hear her slippers scuff across the linoleum floor, and the way she walked so heavily the dishes rattled in the cupboard.

Somehow, in the midst of these tortuous thoughts, Jeanie ate her supper and fled to the rocking chair while Gram finished her meal.

Noisily Gram scraped her chair back and said, "I'll do the dishes. You just get your homework done so you can sew. Land's sake! We should have ordered that material sooner. I don't know where the time is going."

Jeanie had only a theme to write for English. That would go fast. Half an hour later, grateful that she hadn't made an ink blot on it before she finished it, Jeanie clipped the theme into her notebook and put her school books into her bag.

Dreading all that ripping, she went to get the troublesome garment from Gram's dresser. It wasn't in the crumpled heap where she had tossed it. She picked it up—each carefully folded individual piece! Once again Gram had ripped it for her! It was ready to sew again.

Jeanie burst into tears. When she didn't come back to the other room immediately, Gram stuck her head around the corner. "Forgoodnessakes! What are you bawling about? I thought you'd be glad!"

Impulsively, Jeanie flew to her and hugged her. "Oh, I am! I am!" she shouted. "I thought I'd have to spend most of the evening getting it ready to sew again! Thank you!"

Gram gave her a little squeeze. "Well, get at it then, so you're not up half the night!"

Carefully Jeanie matched and basted. Then, controlling the foot treadle with precision, she stitched it. When she examined it, she let out a whoop. Success at last!

She went on to the skirt, sewing seams while mentally composing a letter to Kenny. It was warm enough to write upstairs now. Tonight she would pour it all out—tell him how awful she was, how ugly she felt toward Gram. The guilt of it was simply too heavy to bear any longer.

By the time she was in her quiet room, the words all but wrote themselves.

> Dear Kenny,
> I know you will be shocked, but I have to tell you something I should have told you long ago. I can't stand the guilt any longer. You think I'm so kind and loving, but I'm not! I get terrible ugly, hateful thoughts when Gram does certain things, and I want to run away, or cry or throw something! Can you imagine it? You know how unselfish she is, and how she does everything she can to be helpful to everyone!
> You might as well know what a terrible person I really am. I can't live a lie any longer.

She read what she had written, and suddenly Kenny's face, contorted with shock and disgust, flashed before her eyes. She collapsed in sobs.

Jeanie threw herself on her bed and buried her face in her pillow. She couldn't send that letter! Without Kenny's love, she'd die!

Choking back sobs, she got up and tore it into tiny pieces and began again.

> Dear Kenny,
> One more month and I'll be with you! I'm glad I'm busy sewing. The time will go fast.
> Gram did the nicest thing for me today. . . .

In bed she tried to tell God how sorry she was, but all she could think of was all the kind things Gram had done for her. Her confession seemed totally inadequate. On and on her tortured thoughts raged like the angry waters of a never-ending rapids.

I was a mistake from the very beginning! I've been one huge inconvenience for everyone.

Only one hopeful thought broke through—somewhere, somehow, she'd find the answer to how to keep from feeling so ugly. Maybe she'd find it by getting close to God—like Gram and the people she had read about in Grace Livingston Hill books. Surely that lady hadn't made up how these people felt about God! There must really be a way to know God like that and really love Him instead of just feeing scared of Him.

I want to love You, God! I really do! But I'm afraid of You! I'm so bad and You are so good, and I don't blame You for being disgusted with me. I'll try hard to be better! I'll try as hard as I can tomorrow. Please forgive me for being so ugly today.

With a shuddering sigh she rolled over, utterly exhausted. Sometime . . . someday, maybe she'd be able to smile up at God and not even feel afraid.

"Hey, Ma! I heard yesterday that the current is being turned on this week," Roy told Emma in May. "Soon as I can see my way clear, I'll get a milking machine, and you won't have to feel bad when you can't come and help in the morning."

"Well, it's about time that REA came through!" Emma poured a pail of milk into the strainer on the milk can. "I was reading about milk coolers in the *Wisconsin Agriculturist*. They say if milk is cooled down real fast, it stays fresh much longer."

Roy grinned. "That's right! There'll be lots of changes. I'm going to try to sell the generator and buy a tractor."

"Oh, a tractor would help you so much." In a wistful tone she added, "I do hope you won't get rid of the horses right away, though."

Roy leaned close to her ear. "Oh, no! I'll still use 'em for skidding logs in the woods and a few things here and there. I wouldn't feel right without horses around."

Jeanie was eating breakfast when Emma came in from the barn and shared the news. "*Now* it comes, when I'm almost ready to leave!" Jeanie wailed.

That night she followed Gram around, shouting in her ear while she cooked supper. She had run over to talk with Kenny's mother at noon. "Her sister Minnie will drive us to the train. They'll pick me up, and we'll take the train from Tomahawk."

Although Gram nodded and responded in monosyllables, Jeanie wasn't certain she had heard all she told her. Gram had a way of not hearing what she preferred not to know.

Sure enough, the next evening Gram laid down her knitting to say, "Have you asked Roy about taking you to the train?"

Choking back exasperation, Jeanie shouted, "I told you! Kenny's aunt is picking me up. You know Kenny's mother is going, too!"

"You needn't be so sassy, young lady!" Gram snapped. "I only asked a civil question!"

Jeanie squatted down beside her and grasped her hands. With such little time left, she yearned to make it happy. "Oh, Mama! Remember how I followed you around while you were cooking supper last night and told you all about the plans?"

Gram sighed. "I guess I wasn't listening. I can't keep up with all that jabber!" She looked like she might cry. "Things would have been so different if your mother had lived. She could have taught you so much more than I have."

Jeanie got up and pulled the rocker closer before she answered. "Mama, I'd be lying if I said that I never longed for my mother. But you have taught me so much! I don't see how she could possibly have taught me to care about others more than you have. You always put other people before yourself. I haven't learned how to do that yet, but I think I will as I get older."

Gram blinked back tears. She was having no trouble hearing now!

"And you've taught me is that work is fun, not something to be shunned. You've shown me how exciting it is to see things accomplished. Remember how I'd count the jars of applesauce, string beans, raspberry jam—everything you canned? I loved to line them up on the shelves in the cellar and come up and tell you how many were there.

"And you taught me to enjoy pretty things. Remember the winter you pieced the Rocky Road quilt for me? You let me pick the printed material for each block. I'd come home and see the blocks you had sewn that day and we'd try to decide which were the prettiest. And look how you taught me to sew!"

Gram nodded and smiled. She picked up her knitting, which meant that she had concentrated on listening long enough. "I'm glad I did a few things right!"

There was so much she wanted to talk about with Gram, Jeanie realized as she was getting ready for bed that night. The memory of that awful fight still haunted her.

On Saturday, Jeanie decided to take a walk down by the river. She made her way through the still-muddy pasture down to where Kenny had leaped across the rocks in the river the first time he came out to see her—almost four years ago.

The mere thought of him thrilled her. It would be so wonderful to see him almost every day.

"It's spring!" she said out loud. "It's actually spring!" She had survived the long, lonely winter.

She picked her way across the decayed old log that many feet had trod since the tree had fallen across the creek just above where it flowed into the river. Roy said it had been there before she was born, so it was quite likely that her own mother had walked across it many times. Jeanie walked on up the hill and down the cow path along the river bank.

Peering under the hazel brush, she searched for violets. The tiny green leaf-curls were coming up, but the flowers were far from blooming. Saddened, she retraced her steps and headed back home, ignoring the spring beauties. It was the violets she had come to see.

Gram was on the porch swing when she came back. Everyone else was gone. She sat on Gram's left side.

"I'm going to miss the violets this year!" Jeanie said sadly. "I'm just beginning to realize how many things I'm going to miss."

"No sense thinking about those things," Gram said impatiently. "It's your choice. You don't have to go, you know!"

"But what would I do here if I stayed?"

"Oh, I don't know. You need to get on with your life." Gram sighed. "How I prayed that the Lord would let me live until you were through school. And in a few days you'll graduate."

"But you'll live a long while yet!"

Gram let her knitting rest in her lap. "I hope so. As long as I can be useful I want to live, but if I ever get so I can't take care of myself, I hope the Lord takes me."

"Aren't you afraid to die?"

"Oh forgoodnessakes, no! I know Jesus so well, I think it will be like walking into the next room—and there He'll be!" Her face brightened. "And I'll see Papa and your mother and my sister Anne and my mother. . . ."

Will I ever feel like dying is merely walking through a doorway? Jeanie wondered. *Will I ever feel like I know Jesus that well? Oh, I want to know Him like that!*

For a moment Gram was lost in her thoughts. The only sound was the squeaky old swing. Then, with a start, Gram picked up her knitting, and the needles clicked again.

"I can't imagine how it will be not having to get you up in the morning. Oh, I'd get so angry with you and all your poking around before you finally got going mornings!"

Jeanie leaned close to Gram's left ear. "I'd get pretty angry with you, too!"

"Yes, I suppose you did, but I didn't want to make you angry. Why didn't you tell me when what I was doing made you mad?"

Jeanie made a gesture of futility. "I tried, Mama! I'd get so irritated when you'd say the same things over and over. I'd say, 'You always say that,' but you just kept on doing it."

Gram put her knitting down again. "What did I say over and over?"

Jeanie laughed, a laugh that was half a sob. "Well, for one thing, I couldn't even get both feet through the door before you'd say, 'Now, go put an apron on!'"

Gram nodded. "Yes, I suppose I did. Not easy to get spots out of good clothes, you know. What else did I say all the time?"

For a moment Jeanie couldn't think of another example, though she knew there were a whole string of them. With a wave of her hand she said, "It doesn't matter. You know there were other things that made me even more angry."

Gram nodded. She stopped the swing with her foot and focused her eyes on Jeanie's face as though she had to hear every word.

Jeanie gazed up the hill at the red clay road and the fast-greening fields and took a deep breath. If she was ever going to talk about it, this was the time.

"Mama, why couldn't you ever let me feel good about myself? Whenever someone complimented me, you'd find a way to cancel it out just like that"—she snapped her fingers—"by reminding me of something I had done wrong!"

Jeanie's voice held a sharp edge as she continued to pour out the long years of hurt feelings. "You never praised me for doing something right, but were you always quick to point out my mistakes!" She had lots more to say, but if she started she felt like she might start crying and never stop.

She heard Gram groan. "Oh, my goodness! Girl, that's what mothers are for—to show children where they're wrong!" Gram put her hand gently over Jeanie's. "Don't you see? I couldn't let you become proud! No one likes a haughty person!"

"You think I'm proud!" Jeanie shouted, tears spilling over. "I don't feel like I'm worth anything! According to you, nothing I do is right! How could I possibly be proud?"

Jeanie felt the swing shake. When she glanced over at Gram, she saw she was crying.

"I've thought and thought since—" Gram fumbled for her handkerchief. She turned her tear-streaked face to Jeanie. "I thought I was doing the right thing. I'd never purposely hurt you. You know that, don't you?"

A sparrow chirped in the lilac bush, and Jeanie heard a car rumble across the iron bridge half a mile away.

Gram blew her nose.

Choking back a sob, Jeanie said, "You never said one word when I brought home my report cards full of A's—but you sure noticed those C's I got in typing!"

Gram shook her head. "We were always real careful not to praise the children, because we didn't want them to get proud. We were afraid if they knew how much we loved them, we'd lose control of them."

Jeanie glanced at her pleading eyes and quickly looked away.

"It was so different with you. With the others, I could rely on Papa to back me up—and there were so many in the house I didn't always see what they did wrong. But you ... I felt such a weight of responsibility ... like everyone was watching to see how you'd turn out, and I had to raise you right for your mama's sake."

Jeanie swallowed hard and tried to touch the porch railing with her toe. Gram's helpless anguish was like a cornered wounded animal. For once she was suffering, not Jeanie! The rush of words had released years of pent-up hurt and anger, but now she had a choice— to hold her foot on Gram's neck or to release her.

God! Please help me!

From deep inside came flashes of memories—Gram singling her out from a group with that appealing nod, wink, smile combination, Gram's hearty laughter, Gram's delight in the little ones, Gram's peaceful face as she sat knitting. . . .

With a rush of affection, Jeanie threw her arms around Gram's neck. She felt Gram's stiff body relax, and she returned Jeanie's embrace.

"Oh, dear! Let me get my breath!" Gram said with a laugh that still had a sob of relief in it.

Jeanie released her, but still clung to her hand, trying to convey feelings too deep for words.

Emma shivered. "Brr . . . It's getting cold out here. What's say we have a nice hot cup of tea?"

Jeanie nodded and followed her into the house.

Emma put a stick of wood in the stove and pulled the teakettle over to the front lid. She went to get tea cups and said, "Now, go put an apron—" She stopped, and her eyes met Jeanie's.

Jeanie's irritation vanished. In three steps she had her arms around Gram—and the whole room rang with their laughter.

"Jeanie! Time to get up!"

Gram's loud voice pierced Jeanie's cozy sleep-world. Immediately she swung her left leg out of bed and thumped a response. She drew her leg back and blinked at the golden light on the white ruffled curtains. Through the window she could see the glossy new leaves of the box elder tree nodding in the sunshine. Then, like a dash of cold water, the thought struck her—*This is my last morning at home!*

Tomorrow morning she'd wake up in Chicago at Kenny's sister's apartment. The memory of that dark, narrow street didn't thrill her a bit, but she would see Kenny, and that was all that mattered.

Emma stirred oatmeal into the boiling water and debated. Should she call Jeanie again? Surely she wouldn't poke around this morning. Though Emma's throat ached and her eyes repeatedly filled, she smiled as she realized that those tense mornings of helplessly watching Jeanie run in circles before she made a mad dash for the school bus were over!

On the other hand, the future yawned ahead like an empty cave. No one to cook for. No one to wait for. No one coming home, except for short visits. For the first time in over fifty years, there would be no one depending on her.

What was Jeanie feeling? she wondered. Was she crying, too? Was she wishing she could change her mind?

Emma poured herself a cup of coffee and sat down at the kitchen table, a smile hovering on her lips. No!

Jeanie wouldn't want to turn back . . . nor should she. Emma had seen a good many couples in love in her day—all those private glances, the eyes locked in mutual admiration. These two, she sensed, had something deep and enduring.

Soon Jeanie's thoughts of home would be dim. A whole new life beckoned to her. She was young and bright-eyed and eager to see that blue-eyed young man she loved so much. . . .

Emma closed her eyes and breathed a prayer, committing them to their Heavenly Father's care, and set down her coffee cup with a contented sigh.